CO[illegible] NETWORKING FOR BEGINNERS

A Complete Guide to Network Systems, Wireless Technology, and Cybersecurity. Master the Science of the Internet of Things and Artificial Intelligence

Table of Contents

Introduction

Understanding the concept of computer is a potent endeavor to anyone who seeks to make good use of networking resources and services; in the current world where networking in all aspects of human interaction is heavily linked to the use of computers. From social networking through to digital media and business networking, the world has indeed become a global village thanks to the trillion-dollar idea of PC networking. In everything that we do, it is unavoidable to mention the Internet as the biggest fruit of PC networking. With a lot of strides having been made in computer networking, communication systems are becoming more and more efficient day in, day out.

In Computer Networking, readers get to familiarize themselves with the fundamental aspects of computer networking, starting with the very basic networking nitty-gritty that primarily aim at setting the tempo towards more advanced concepts of computer networking. Though briefly explained, the information provided for every topic is sufficiently covered to suffice the essential needs of a networking beginner.

The first chapter introduces the reader to the basic concepts of computers that include a simple description of a computer network, network topology, and network types. In addition, there is also a brief overview of wireless networks as well as a deep discussion of network security.

In subsequent chapters, other important networking topics come to the fore, including wireless technology, peer-to-peer networking, router, server basics, and IP addressing. Internet basics and functions are also covered with special attention on the World Wide Web. Furthermore, the book explores an overview of the CCNA course coverage as well as the essentials of machine learning.

The book introduces the reader to the exciting networking experience: it stirs up readers' curiosity to venture further into the more advanced coverage of computer networking by offering a firm foundation in the larger field of PC networking.

Chapter 1: An Introduction to Computer Networking

Networking Essentials

What Is a Computer Network?

Computer network is a term that refers to any group of computers that are linked to one another, allowing for communication among them. A network also allows member computers to share applications, data, and other network resources (file servers, printers, and many others).

Computer networks may be differentiated according to size, functionality, and even location. However, size is the main criterion with which computer networks are classified. Thus, there are a number of unique computer networks that we shall discuss individually under the subtopic Types of Computer Networks.

Network Topologies

A network topology refers to the arrangement and the way components of a network are interconnected. There are two forms of computer network topologies.

Logical Topology

Logical topology defines how linked network devices appear in a network. It is the architectural design of a network's communication mechanism among the different devices.

Physical Topology

Physical topology can be said to be the way all the nodes of a network are geometrically represented. The following are the various types of physical topologies:

Bus Topology

In this topology, all hosts on a network are linked via a single cable. Network devices are either linked directly to the backbone cable or via drop cables.

When a node wants to relay some message, it relays it to the entire network. The message is received by all the network nodes regardless of whether it is addressed or not.

This topology is primarily adopted for 802.4 and 802.3 (Ethernet) standard networks.

Bus topology configuration is simpler in comparison with other topologies.

The backbone cable is a "single lane" through which messages are relayed to all the nodes on the network.

Bus topologies popularly rely on CSMA as the primary access method.

CSMA is a media access control that regulates data flow in order to maintain data integrity over the network.

Advantages of Bus Topology

- The cost of installation is low since nodes are interconnected directly using cables without the need for a hub or switch.

- Support for moderate data speeds by use of coaxial and twisted pair cables that allows up to 10 Mbps only.

- Uses familiar technology that makes its installation and troubleshooting a walk in the park, since tools and materials are readily available.

- There is a great degree of reliability since the failure of a single node does have no effect on the rest of the network nodes.

Disadvantages of Bus Topology

- Cabling is quite extensive. This may make the process quite tedious.

- Troubleshooting for cable failures is mostly a pain to most network administrators.

- Chances of message collision are high in case different nodes send messages simultaneously.

- The addition of new nodes slows down the entire network.
- Expansion of the network causes attenuation-loss of signal strength. This may be corrected with the use of repeaters (to regenerate the signal).

Ring Topology

The only difference between ring topology and bus topology is that in the former, the ends are connected, while in the former, ends are open.

When one node gets a message from the sender, that node sends the message to the next node. Hence, communication takes place in one direction-it is unidirectional

Each and every single node on the network is linked to another node without a termination point. Data flows continuously in one loop-endless loop.

Data flow always takes a clockwise direction.

Ring topology often uses *token passing* as the main access method.

Token passing: an access method in which tokens are passed from station to another.

Token: a data frame that moves around the network.

Token Passing in Action

- A token moves around the network from one node to another till the destination.
- The sender puts an address plus data in the token.
- The token passes from one node to the next-checking the token address against the individual addresses of each and every node on the network until it finds a match.
- The token is used as a carrier-for data (and the destination address).

Merits of Ring Topology

- Network management is relatively easy since faulty components can be removed without interfering with the others.

- Most of the hardware and software requirements for this network topology are readily available.
- The installation cost is quite low since the popular twisted pair cables that required in plenty are quite inexpensive.
- The network is largely reliable since it does not rely on a single host machine.

Demerits of Ring Topology

- Troubling may be quite a task in the absence of specialized test equipment. Detection of a fault in the cable is normally a serious challenge.
- Failure in one node leads to failure in the entire network since tokens have to through each node for a complete cycle of communication from sender to destination.
- The addition of new network devices slows down the entire network.
- Communication delay increases with increasing nodes/network components.

Star Topology

In this topology, a central computer, switch or hub connects all the nodes on the network. The central device is the server while the peripherals are clients.

Coaxial cables or Ethernet's RJ-45 are favored for connection of the network nodes to the server. Switches are hubs are preferred as the main connection devices in this topology.

This is by far the most widely used topology in network implementations.

Pros of Star Topology

- There is the ease of troubleshooting since problems are handled at individual stations.
- Complex network control features can be implemented with ease at the server side-which also allows the automation of certain tasks.
- There's a limited failure since an issue in one cable does not translate into an entire network problem. The fault in a cable may only affect a single node on the network since the nodes are not interconnected via cables.

- Open ports on a switch or hub allow for easy expansion of the network.
- The use of inexpensive coaxial cables makes star topology highly cost-effective to implement.
- It has the capacity to handle the data speed of up to 100Mbps. Hence, it supports data transmission at very high speeds.

Cons of Star Topology

- If the central connecting device fails or malfunctions, then the entire network goes down.
- The use of cabling at times makes routing an exhausting exercise-cable routing is normally difficult.

Tree Topology

This topology puts the features of bus and star topologies in one basket.

In this topology, all computers are interconnected, but in a hierarchical manner.

The top-most node in this topology is referred to as a *root node*, whereas all the others are descendants of the root node.

There exists just a single path between two nodes for the transmission of data-forming a parent-child hierarchy.

Merits of Tree Topology

- It supports broadband data transmission over long distances without issues of attenuation.

- Star topology allows for easy expansion of a network since new devices can be added without an existing network with little difficulty.

- Ease of management-networks are segmented into star networks that make it relatively easy to manage.

- Errors can be detected and corrected with ease.

- Malfunctioning or breakdown of a single node does not affect the other nodes on the network. Thus, there is a limited failure on tree topology networks.

- It supports point-to-point wiring of each and every network segment.

Demerits of Tree Topology

- It is always difficult to handle issues in respect of a fault in a node.
- It's a high-cost network topology since broadband transmission can cost an arm and a leg.
- Failure or faults in the main bus cable affects the entire network.
- There is difficulty in reconfiguring the network when new devices are added onto the network.

Mesh Topology

All computers are interconnected via redundant connections in this topology. It offers different (multiple) paths from one node to another.

In mesh topology, there are no connecting devices like switches or hub—for instance, the internet.

WANs normally are implemented with mesh topology since communication failures are of serious concern. It is also largely implemented in wireless networks.

The formula for forming mesh topology is shown below:

Number of Cables = (z*(z-1))/2

Where;

z = the number of nodes on the network

There are 2 categories of this topology:

Partially Connected Mesh

In this topology, not all the network devices are linked to the devices with which they have frequent communications. The devices are only connected to some of the devices with which they are normally in constant communication.

Full Mesh Topology

Each network device has a link to every other device in the network in a full-mesh topology. In simple words, all computers are connected to one another via redundant connections.

Merits of Mesh Topology

- Mesh topologies are highly reliable since a breakdown in one single connection does not affect the working of the nodes in the network.

- Communication is fast since each computer has connections with all other computers on the network.

- The addition of new devices has no effect on other devices on the network-making reconfiguration quite easy.

Demerits of Mesh Topology

- Mesh topology networks has the capacity to accommodate more devices and transmission media than any other network topology. This translates to a high cost of setting up mesh networks than all other networks.

- Mesh topology networks are normally too large to manage and maintain effectively.

- A lot of redundancy on the network reduces the network efficiency significantly.

Hybrid Topology

The amalgamation of different network topologies (at least two of them) results in another topology that is conventionally referred to as a hybrid topology. It is a connection between different links and computers for data transmission.

A hybrid can only be formed by a combination of dissimilar topologies. For instance, a combination of bus and star topologies. However, a combination of similar topologies does result in a hybrid topology.

Advantages of Hybrid Topology

- An issue in one part of the network does not mess with the entire network.
- Hybrid topology allows the network to be scaled further by the addition of more devices without messing with the existing network.
- This network topology is quite flexible. An organization can customize the nature of its network to suit its specific network needs and interests.
- The network topology is highly effective since it can be designed in a way that network strength is maximized, and the limitations of the network are minimized.

Disadvantages of Hybrid Topology

- The network topology is quite complex. Thus, it is too difficult to come up with a suitable architectural design of a network.

It is highly costly since hubs used in this sort of computer network are different from the ordinary hubs. The hubs used in this topology are more expensive. Besides, the overall infrastructure is highly costly since a lot of cabling is required a plus many more network devices.

Networks Types

The following are the four major classifications of computer networks based on size:

Local Area Network (or simply, LAN)

A LAN refers to any group of computers that are linked to one another, a small area like an office or a small building. In a LAN, two or more computers are connected via communication media like coaxial cables, twisted pair cable, or fiber-optic cable.

It is easy and less costly to set up a LAN since it can do just fine with inexpensive network hardware such as switches, Ethernet cables and network adapters. The limited traffic allows for faster transmission of data over LANs.

Besides, LANs are easy to manage since they are set up in a small space. Thus, even security enforcement is also enhanced through closer monitoring of activities within the network's geographical location.

Personal Area Network (PAN)

This network is arranged and managed in the space of its user(s)-normally a range not exceeding 10m. It is typically used to connect computer devices for personal use.

Components of a personal area network include a laptop, mobile phone, media player devices as well as play stations. Such components are located within an area of about 30ft of a person's space.

The idea of PANs was born by one Thomas Zimmerman—the first lead research scientist to conceive the idea of personal area networks.

There are 2 classes of PANSs:

Wired PANs: a wired personal area network is created when a person uses a USB cable to connect two different hardware devices. For instance, it is a common practice nowadays to connect a phone to a computer via a USB cable to share files, access the Internet, and many other things.

Wireless PANs: a wireless PAN is set up by the use of existing wireless technologies such as Bluetooth and Wi-Fi. This is basically a low-range technology network type.

Examples of PANs

There are three common types of personal area networks:

1. **Body Area Network:** it moves with an individual. A good example is a mobile network-when one establishes a network connection and then makes a connection with a different device within their range.

2. **Offline Network:** it is also called a home network. It can be set up in a home-linked computer, TV, printers and phones-but is not connected to the internet.

3. **Small Home Office Network:** different devices are connected to the Internet and corporate network via VPN.

Metropolitan Area Network (or simply, MAN)

A MAN is a type of network that extends over a larger geographical area by different interconnecting LANs to form a bigger network of computers. Thus, it covers a wider area than a LAN.

MANs are ideally set up in cities and big towns. Hence, the name metropolitan area network. It is often used by government agencies to connect with citizens some big institutions; communication among banking institutions within a given city; in big institutions of higher learning located in a metropolis; and even used for communication in military bases within a city/town.

The commonly adopted Metropolitan area network protocols include Frame Relay, ISDN, RS-232, ADSL, ATM, and OC-3, among others.

Wide Area Network (or simply, WAN)

This is a network that stretches over large geographical regions-cities, states, and even countries. It is bigger than LAN or MAN. It is not restricted to a particular geographical location. It spans over large geographical locations by the use of telephone lines, satellite links, or fiber optic cables. The Internet is a perfect example among the existing WANs globally.

WANs are widely embraced for education, government, and business activities.

WAN Examples

Mobile Broadband: 3G or 4G networks are widely serving people in a big region, state or even country.

Private Network: banks create private networks that link different offices established in different locations via a telephone leased line that's obtained from a telecom company.

Last Mile: telecommunication companies offer internet services to thousands of customers in different cities by simply connecting homes, offices a and business premises with fiber.

Advantages of WANs

- WANs cover large geographical locations reaching out to masses of the human population. The impact of the Internet in people's lives globally sums up the advantages of a wide area network.
- Centralized data: WANs support the centralization of data/information. This eliminates a need for individuals to buy back-up servers for their e-mails and files.

- Getting updated files: programmers get updated files within seconds since software work on live servers.
- A quick exchange of message: WANs use technologies and sophisticated tools that enable message exchange to happen faster than on most other networks. Communication via Skype and Facebook are two good examples of quick message exchange, thanks to the internet one of the popular WANs in the world.
- WANs allow the sharing of resources and software. It is possible to share hard drives, RAM, and other resources via wide area networks.
- Business without borders: presently, even people separated by the Pacific can still conduct thriving business without moving an inch from their current location because of the Internet. The world is indeed a global village.
- High bandwidth: use of leased lines for companies increases bandwidth. This in turn increases data transfer rates, thereby increasing the productivity of the company.

Disadvantages of WANs

- Security issues are escalated as the network size increases. Thus, the issue of insecurity is of more concern on a WAN than it is on a LAN or MAN.
- High installation cost: setting a WAN requires the purchase of much costly equipment as well as software applications to manage and administer the network. Routers, switches and mainframe computers that are needed to serve the network all cost a fortune.
- Network troubleshooting is often a big concern since the network spans large geographical locations.

Neural networks

A neural network refers to a set of algorithms that are used for pattern recognition. The algorithms are loosely molded after the brains of humans.

Neural networks are most crucial in the interpretation of sensory data via machine perception, clustering, and labelling raw data.

A neural network recognizes numerical patterns that are found in vectors. All data-time series, images, text and sound-are translated in the vectors.

Functions of Neural Networks

The following are the 3 most vital roles that can be performed by neural networks:

Classification: Labeled data sets are the key factors in any classification. Humans have to transfer their own knowledge to the labeled dataset so as to enable a neural network to get the correlation data and the labels in a process known as supervised learning.

A neural network can achieve the following classification tasks:

- Face detection, people identification in images, and recognition of facial expressions.
- Object identification in images.
- Voice recognition, speech transcription into text, sentiment recognition in voice, and speaker identification (in a dialogue/conversation).
- Text classification-fraudulent text in insurance claims and spam in e-mails.

Clustering: This is also referred to as grouping. It involves the detection of similarities. This can be achieved without labeling in a process known as unsupervised learning. The process involves the following:

- Search: images, documents, or sounds are compared to obtain related items.
- Detection of anomalies: clustering also seeks to detect unusual behavior among grouped data. This is highly essential in the detection and prevention of certain undesirable items and activities such as fraud.

Predictive Analysis: this is commonly known as regression.

Deep learning relies on data classification for the establishment of correlations between objects. This can be simply be referred to as static prediction.

Deep learning has the ability to establish correlations between current and future events.

Predictive analysis is most crucial when it comes to the following:

- Health breakdowns.
- Customer churn.
- Hardware breakdowns.
- Employee turnover.

Elements of a Neural Network

Deep learning is another term for 'stacked neural networks.'

Stacked neural networks are networks that are made up of a number of layers.

Each network layer is made up of different nodes-a computational point patterned on the neuron of the brain of a human.

A node puts together all data inputs with the weights (set of coefficients). The weights can either dampen or amplify the input. This, in turn, gives significance to the inputs that concern the task on which a given algorithm is trying to pick up.

In summary, the following are the key elements of a neural network:

- Layers.

- Nodes.
- Set of coefficients (weights).

The OSI Model

OSI is a short form for Open System Interconnection. The model offers a description of the way information and data from a software application is transmitted through physical media to another software application in a totally unrelated computer.

This reference model is comprised of seven layers. Each layer has a specific role to play.

The OSI Reference model was born in 1984 by the International Organization (ISO). In modern days, this is taken to be the basic architectural model for communication between different network hosts.

In the OSI model, whole tasks are broken down into seven smaller and manageable chunks. Layers are assigned distinct roles-each layer is assigned a specific task to handle. Also, each layer is sufficiently equipped to handle its tasks independently.

Features of the OSI Model

The OSI model is broadly divided into two layers: upper and lower layers.

The upper layer of this model primarily handles issues related to applications. Those issues are executed in the software. The layer that is closest (or the uppermost layer) to the user is the application layer. The end-user interacts with software applications just as the application software does.

When a layer is said to be an upper layer, it is said so in reference to another. An upper layer is a layer that lies right above the other one.

The lower layer of this model handles issues of data transport. The implementation of the data link, as well as physical layers, occurs in software and hardware. In this model, the physical layer stands as the lowest layer. It is also the nearest to the physical medium. Primarily, the physical layers provide the necessary information to the physical medium.

Roles of the 7 Layers of the OSI Model

We're going to focus on the functions of the unique layers of the OSI Reference model from the lowest to the uppermost.

Physical Layer

- **Data Transmission:** it defines the mode of transmission between two network devices- whether it is the full-duplex, half-duplex, or simplex mode.
- **Line Configuration**: it offers a clear definition of the way two or more network devices are physically linked.
- **Signals**: the physical layer determines the nature of signals used to transmit information.
- **Topology**: the physical layer offers a comprehensive definition of the arrangement of network devices.

Data Link Layer

This layer is charged with the task of ensuring error-free data transfer of data frames over the network. It also defines data format on the network.

The data link layer ensures that there is a reliable and efficient inter-network device communication. It is responsible for the unique identification of each device that is found on the network.

Data link layer comprises of the following two layers:

1. **Logical link control layer:** it transfers packets to the destination's network layer. Besides, it identifies the specific address of the network layer of the receiver from the packet header. Furthermore, flow control is implemented in this layer.

2. **Media Access Control Layer:** this refers to a link that exists between the physical layer and link control layer. This is what transfers data packets over a network.

The Data Link Layer's Actual Functions

- **Framing**: the data link layer does the translation of the physical layer's raw bitstream into data packets referred to as frames. It adds a header and trailer to the data frame. The header contains both the destination and source addresses.

- **Physical addressing:** the physical addressing layer enjoins a header to the frame. This header has the address of the receiver. The frame is relayed to the receiver whose address is indicated on the header.

- **Data Flow control:** this is the data link layer's primary role. It maintains a constant data rate so that no data is corrupted while on transit.

- **Error control:** this is achieved by the addition of a cyclic redundant check (CRC) on the trailer that is put onto the data packet before being sent to the physical layer. In case of any errors, the receiver can request for the retransmissions of the corrupted frame.

- **Access control:** this layer determines which of the available network devices is given top priority over the link at a particular moment.

The Network Layer

This is number 3 on the 7-layer OSI Reference model. It handles device addressing and keeps track of device location on the network. Based on network conditions, the layers determine the most favorable path for data transfer from sender to receiver. Another condition that is considered in determining the best path is service priority, among others.

This layer is charged with the responsibility of routing and forwarding packets. Routers are some of the devices on layer 3. The routers are specified in the network layer and are used to offer routing services in a computer internetwork.

Protocols that are used in the routing of network traffic include IPv6 and IP.

Network Layer Functions

- **Addressing**: this layer ensures that the destination and source addresses are added to the header of the frame. Addressing is helpful in the identification of devices on a network.
- **Internetworking**: the network layer offers a logical link between network devices.
- **Packetizing**: the network layer receives frames from upper layers and turns them into packets in a process that is conventionally referred to as packetizing. It is realized by the Internet protocol.

The Transport Layer

This is layer number 4 in the model.

The layer ensures that it follows the order, in which they are sent. It makes sure that duplication of data does not occur. This layer's core business is to ensure that data is transferred totally.

The physical layer receives data from the upper layers and subdivides them further into smaller chunks that are referred to as segments.

The layer provides communication between destination and source-from end to end- for data reliability. It can also be termed as end-to-end layer.

There are two protocols that are implemented at this layer:

Transmission Control Protocol

This is a standard protocol that allows systems to share messages/information over the internet. The protocol establishes and preserves the link between hosts.

TCP divides data into smaller units referred to as segments. The resulting segments do not travel over the internet using the same route. They reach the destination in no specific. However, TCP reorders the individual segments at the destination to reconstitute the original message.

User Datagram Protocol (or simply, UDP)

This is also a transport layer protocol. As opposed to what happens in TCP, the source does not receive any acknowledgment when the destination receives data. This renders the protocol quite unreliable.

Transport Layer Functions

- **Service-point Addressing:** service-point addressing enables computers to run multiple applications simultaneously. It also allows data transmission to the receiver not only from one machine to another machine but also from one process to the next process. The transport layer adds a port address or service-point address to the packet.

  Whereas the network does the transmission of data from one machine to another, it is the transport layer that ensures data transmission to the appropriate processes.

- **Segmentation and reassembly:** this layer receives a message from its upper layer. It then splits the whole message into several small chunks. The layer assigns sequence numbers to each segment for identification.

  At the receiving end, the transport layer reconstitutes the segments based on the sequence numbers to form the original message.

- **Connection control:** there are 2 services that the transports offer: connectionless service and connection-based.

  A connectionless service considers each segment to be a distinct packet. The packets travel through different routes to the destination. On the other hand, the connection-based service makes a connection with the destination machine's transport for before packets are delivered. In the connection-based service, all packets move in a single route.

- **Error control:** Just like in data control, this is achieved on an end-to-end basis-not across a single link. The transport layer at the source ensures that the message gets to its destination error-free.

- **Flow control:** this layer also ensures data control. The data control is done from end to end, but not across one dedicated link.

The Session Layer

This layer is used for the establishment, maintenance, and synchronization of interaction between communicating network devices.

Session Layer Functions

- **Dialog control:** this layer serves as a dialog controller. The layer achieves by initiating dialog between two processes. Alternatively, the layer can be said to authorize communication between one process and another. This can either be half-duplex or full-duplex.

- **Synchronization:** the session layer adds checkpoints in a sequence during data transmission. In case of errors along the way, retransmission of data takes place from the specific checkpoint. The entire process is referred to as synchronization and recovery.

The Presentation Layer

This layer primarily deals with the language and formatting of information that is transferred between two network devices. It is the network's "translator."

The presentation layer is a section of the operating system. It is the portion of the operating system that makes the conversation of data from a given presentation format to another presentation format.

This layer is also referred to as the syntax layer.

Role of the Presentation Layer

- **Translation**: Processes in different systems exchange information as to character numbers, character strings, and many more. Different encoding techniques are applied on different computing machines. It is the presentation layer that handles interoperability between then, unlike encoding techniques.

  The layer does the conversion of data from the sender-based formats into common formats into receiver-dependent formats at the destination computers.

- **Encryption**: The presentation layer performs encryption to ensure the privacy of data.

  Encryption is the process that involves the conversion of information transmitted from the sender into another unique form that is then transmitted over the network.

- **Compression**: the presentation compresses data before its transmission. The compression involves the reduction of the number of bits. This process is essential, especially in the transmission of multimedia such as video and audio files.

The Application Layer

This layer offers the interface for users and applications to access resources on the network. It handles network issues like resource allocation, transparency, and many more. This is not an application. It simply plays its application layer role. It provides network services to end-users.

Application Layer Functions

- **Access, transfer, and management of files:** this layer allows users to access files remotely, retrieve them, and still manage them remotely.

- **Mail services:** this layer offers e-mail storage and forwarding storage facility.
- **Directory services:** this layer offers the distributed database bases. This is essential in the provision of important information about different objects.

Computer Network Components

These comprise of network hardware and network software components that constitute a computer network. In this section, we're typically concerned with the major hardware components that are crucial for the installation of a computer network.

Computer network components include computers, cables, network interface cards (NIC), switches, modems, hubs, and routers.

Computers

Computers may be desktop computers, laptops as well as portable devices (smartphones and tablets) plus their additional accessories such as portable hard drives, CD Players, keyboards, and mice. They are the major hardware components of any computer network.

Computers are the primary components without which a network is just but a dream. Computers offer the platform for users to perform their different tasks on the network. In the case of a centralized system, computers serve as a link between users and the dedicated network server.

The Network Interface Card

The NIC (as it is commonly called) is a hardware component that links one computer to another on the same network.

The NIC supports network transfer rates from 10Mbps through to 1000Mbps.

All network cards have a unique address assigned by the IEEE. These unique addresses are referred to as the physical/MAC addresses and are used to recognize each computer on the network.

There are two unique forms of network cards: Wireless and Wired NICs.

Hub

A hub divides a network connection into several devices. A hub connects all computers on a network via cables.

Every computer sends a request to the network through the hub.

When the hub gets a request from a particular computer, it broadcasts that request across the network to all network devices.

Each network device checks the request to determine if it belongs there. If not, the request is subsequently discarded.

The downside to this process is the consumption of more bandwidth, and communication is highly limited. Presently, a hub is as good as obsolete due to the hype with routers and switches.

Switch

A switch links a number of devices on a computer network. This important connection device is technologically more advanced than a hub.

A switch has an update that determines the destination of transmitted data. The switch transmits a message to the desired destination as per the physical address on each incoming request.

Unlike the hub, it does not transmit data to all devices across the network. Thus, there is an increased data transmission speed since individual computers communicate directly with the switch.

Router

A router gives an internet connection to a local area network. It receives, analyzes, and forwards incoming packets to another computer network.

It operates in Layer three of the OSI Reference model- simply referred to as the network layer.

Packet forwarding is based on the information contained in the routing table. A router is smart enough to choose or decide the most appropriate path for the transmission of data from all available paths.

Modem

A modem is an acronym that stands for Modulator/Demodulator. It changes digital data into analog signals over a telephone line.

The modem makes it possible for a computer to establish a connection to the Internet via an existing telephone line. It is installed on the PCI slot of the motherboard-not on the motherboard itself.

Connectors and Cables

A cable is a physical transmission medium that is used to transmit a signal.

The cables used for transmission include the coaxial cables, twisted pair cables, and fiber optic cables.

Testing the Network Wiring

The first step to test the network wiring is to make a chart to help keep track of the testing progress. A floor plan showing where the wires are or a room-by-room listing will work fine. Check each one off when it tests okay.

Once the chart is done, get someone to help you, posting that person at the distant end of the cable from you. In a large building, use two-way handheld radios or cell phones to communicate; this will move the testing project along faster.

To test your cables, use a cable tester or if you don't have a cable tester, a volt-ohm meter. If you are going to test a lot of end-point jacks, then borrow or invest in a cable tester. When the connections are good, with all four pairs of wires in the cable conducting properly, lights will illuminate on both ends of the tester. Having this tester makes checking a large number of cables, an easy job.

If you opt to use a volt-ohm meter, you will need to build a patch cable that can be used to sort out the respective pairs on one end of the cable run so you can check for continuity on the other end. A shorting cord for the distant end of the cable connects together the appropriate pairs on RJ-11 or RJ-12 or on the Ethernet connector.

If you are going to use this more primitive method instead of a cable tester, you will need three shorted patch cables; one four-position plug will work for RJ-11 and 12. If you have RJ-25s, you will need to test them with a 6P6C plug; to test Ethernet cables, you will need an 8P8C plug with the appropriate pairs shorted out. You will then to need to fabricate another plug and patch cord with the wire stripped back 1/2 inch for connecting to the leads on the ohmmeter. Each pair should trigger the alarm on the continuity check or just read a few ohms of resistance, which will vary with distance. The resistance reading should not exceed 19.7 ohms over 100 meters of cable length.

Basic Network Troubleshooting

Network troubleshooting refers to all the measures and techniques assembled to identify, diagnose, and resolve network issues. The process is systematic and primarily seeks to restore normalcy to the functionality of a computer network.

Network administrators are charged with the responsibility of identifying network problems and repairing it with the aim of ensuring a smooth run of operations in the network. They also do whatever it takes to ensure that the network is operating at optimal levels.

The following are among the many computer network troubleshooting processes:

- Configuration and re-configuration of switches, routers, or any other network component.
- Identifying any network issues and figuring out a way to fix it.
- Installation and repair of network cables as well as Wi-Fi devices.
- Get rid of malware from the network.

- Get firmware devices up to date.
- Installation and uninstallation of software as is necessary.

Network troubleshooting can be done manually or as an automated task-especially when it has to do with network software applications. Network diagnostic software is a valuable tool when it comes to the identification of network issues that may not be easy to detect with the human eye.

Network troubleshooting includes both hardware troubleshooting and software troubleshooting.

Hardware Troubleshooting

This is a form troubleshooting that takes care of issues with hardware components. It may include:

- Removal of faulty or damaged RAM, hard disk or NIC.
- The dusting of computers and other network devices-dust accumulation sometimes leads to malfunctioning of devices.

- Tightening of cables that connect different network components.
- Updating or installation of important hardware drivers.

Hardware troubleshooting begins with the discovery of a given hardware issue, the cause, and finally, taking the necessary remedial action.

Software Troubleshooting

Software entails a set of measures for scanning, recognizing, diagnosing, and offering solutions to issues with software in the network. It includes issues with network operating systems, diagnostic software as well as software applications installed on individual network computers.

Chapter 2: Network Management

Effective network management must address all issues pertaining to the following:

- Hardware.
- Administration and end-user support.
- Software.
- Data management.

Hardware Management and Maintenance

Hardware maintenance can be performed as per the following routines and considerations:

Cleaning

Every two weeks, clean all network equipment. Doing so will help keep your equipment cool and make other maintenance tasks easier to perform. When cleaning, dust the equipment, shelves, and nearby areas. A small vacuum should be used to vacuum keyboards and the computer vent and fan openings. Additionally, you should use the vacuum to gently suck dust out of removable media drives. Unused wall jacks and empty equipment jacks in dust-prone environments can be vacuumed on occasion as well.

For printers and plotters, follow the manual instructions for cleaning print heads on inkjets and vacuuming paper dust from laser printers. Monitors can be wiped down with an eye-glass cleaning solutions and glasses-cleaning cloths.

Performing Inspections

Keeping a close eye on the condition of all hardware is essential. For this reason, you should inspect all hardware at least once per month. This inspection should include the following:

- Make sure cooling vents are not blocked or excessively dusty.
- Listen to and feel the vents to make sure cooling fans are operating.
- Sniff the area. When power supplies and other parts are near failing, they may emit an odd odor from excessive heating. A burnt smell means trouble is imminent or has already occurred.
- Check all power cables, peripheral cables, and network cables for tightness in their sockets.
- Check all power cables, peripheral cables, and network cables for fraying or other damage.
- Check the server area for proper operation of heating, venting, and cooling systems to be sure they are operable- even if those systems are not needed at the time of the inspections.

Upgrading Firmware

"Firmware" refers to any program that is resident in a chip. For example, a computer's BIOS is the firmware. Sometimes, manufacturers release updates for the firmware to fix flaws or to enable the equipment to work with some newly released hardware device or operating-system upgrade. You should check the manufacturer's Web site or help desk for all network equipment at least quarterly to determine whether any firmware upgrades are available for your equipment.

If so, be sure to adhere to the maker's instructions to the letter for loading new firmware and firmware updates. Firmware loads often require low-level booting from a DOS or maintenance disk, although some will be compatible with the computer's operating system.

Upgrading Hardware

Two factors drive hardware upgrades:

- Performance issues due to changes in applications or the addition of new applications may necessitate a hardware upgrade or the addition of new features that are linked to the hardware's capability or capacity. For example, adding memory and installing an additional hard drive for more file space are typical upgrades performed to support those changes.

- You may opt to upgrade hardware on a purely optional basis-for example, adding a bigger monitor, higher-quality sound card, a TV card, or a similar device.

Repairing Hardware

As the person responsible for the network, you must assess your willingness and ability to perform hardware repairs-before a hardware component stops working. To that end, you should go through your entire hardware inventory and determine the following:

- Is the equipment still under warranty? If so, take advantage of that warranty in the event the equipment stops working.

- Would it be more cost-effective to simply replace a piece of hardware if it breaks? Given the high cost of technical labor, repairing a low-cost item, such as a printer that can be replaced for $50, may not be justified. It might even be best to replace rather than repair PCs purchased for less than $600 if you've used them for more than ten months. Don't get me wrong: I am not advocating short equipment life cycles or unnecessarily adding to scrap piles.

- For big-ticket items, you may want to transfer the repair risk to someone else by arranging for service and support contracts-assuming your budget can support this.

Administration

Large networks often have one or more staff members dedicated exclusively to performing network administrative tasks. For smaller networks, the manager must wear various hats and perform multiple roles to support the network. Over time, he or she must rise to the level of journeyman-or at least experienced apprentice-to be successful.

Primary or routine network-administrative tasks fall into one of the following categories:

- Administering and supporting end-users.
- Adding workstations and peripheral devices.
- Maintaining system-wide documentation.

Maintaining System-Wide Documentation

Maintaining system-wide documentation might seem like a task you could skip, but you shouldn't. Without complete documentation, a lot of person-ours can be wasted when something goes wrong, or when you are trying to add hardware to a server or applications to network hosts or workstations. Regrettably, for some technicians and network managers, checking the documentation prior to making system changes is not a priority one as it should be. Good documentation practices are not a bane because they take time; they are a benefit to the network manager with little time to waste.

Network documentation should include all operation and maintenance booklets as well as manuals for all the hardware.

Administering and Supporting End Users

As the network administrator, you will likely be responsible for administering and supporting end-users. Examples of tasks you'll need to perform may include the following:

- Vetting new users for security purposes.

- Adding, deleting, and changing end-user accounts.
- Creating and administering group, role-based, and individual access controls.
- Providing technical support.
- Adding workstations and peripheral devices.

Adding Workstations and Peripheral Devices

There will likely be times when some software-based administrative chores must be completed in order to add new workstations and peripheral devices to the network. Examples are hardcoding an IP address into a new workstation or printer or attaching a new printer to a print server's queue. In addition, users may need to be assigned rights to access new equipment such as printers, along with access passwords for new workstations on the network. For more information, consult the documentation provided with the new equipment and your own documentation of necessary steps from previous changes.

Virtualization in Cloud Computing

What is cloud computing?

Cloud computing refers to the delivery of IT resources via the internet as per the demand. It is normally implemented on a pay-as-you-go pricing basis. The concept of cloud computing seeks to offer a solution to users' needs of IT infrastructure at a low cost.

Why cloud computing?

For small as well as big IT companies that still rely on traditional methods to operate primarily require a server to carry out their different tasks. The setting up of a server room requires skilled personnel, different servers, modems, switches, and lots of other networking resources-plus a lot more of other non-IT requirements that contribute to the completeness of a working office.

Traditional methods require a lot of human input, expensive equipment, and a lot of other logistical necessities. These things require large sums of money. In order to set up a fully functional server, the organization or individual must be willing to break the bank. However, that is no longer thanks to the concept of cloud computing. Cloud computing helps individuals to cut down on infrastructure costs by eliminating the need for the purchase of expensive equipment and spending a lot of funds on hired personnel for the administration and management of IT resources.

Features of Cloud Computing

- Cloud computing operates in a distributed computing environment. This makes resource sharing to happen quickly.
- Cloud computing minimizes the chances of infrastructure failure due to the existence of many servers. This makes it a more reliable infrastructure for IT operations.
- Cloud computing allows for the large-scale, on-demand provision of IT resources without the need for engineers and many other professional that would otherwise come in handy.
- Cloud computing enables multiple users to share resources and work more efficiently by sharing the same infrastructure.
- Cloud computing eliminates physical location or distance concerns since users can access systems and resources regardless of their geographic location.

- Maintaining cloud computing applications is easier since they do not need to be installed on each user's computer.
- Cloud computing reduces the operating cost of an organization since it eliminates the organization's need to set up its own infrastructure-this turns out to be quite an expensive undertaking for most organizations. Besides, it allows an organization to only pay for a service or resource when needed.
- Cloud computing allows for pay-per-use mode for different services. It is a convenient way to use, especially when a user needs to use a resource only once.

Benefits of Cloud Computing

The following are the major benefits of cloud computing:

- A person can conveniently use a low-cost computer to perform complex computer tasks that would otherwise require powerful machines-machines that fetch high prices in the market. Applications run on a cloud, not on the user's machine.

- Low-cost IT infrastructure is can sufficiently meet an organization's needs. There is no need of invest in high-cost IT infrastructure to handle big servers.
- Low-cost maintenance due to reduced infrastructural requirements-in terms of hardware and software.
- Instant software updates for web-based applications-no need to worry about obsolete applications and high upgrade costs.
- The execution capacity of cloud servers is very high. These increases computing power and leads to efficient task execution due to high speeds of data processing and message delivery
- A cloud provides users with very large storage capacities-at very low costs.

Disadvantages of Cloud Computing

Some of the most conspicuous limitations of cloud computing are listed below:

- You cannot access resources on a cloud without internet connectivity. It is mandatory that the user is connected to the internet in order to access resources (or use the IT infrastructure) offered on a cloud.
- Low internet connectivity may be greatly frustrating when trying to perform important tasks on a cloud. Most web-based applications run effectively on a lot of bandwidth. Low bandwidth may, at times, cripple the execution of some tasks.
- There is no guarantee of security and confidentiality of data stored on a cloud. Unauthorized users can gain access to your data/information stored on a cloud.

What is virtualization?

Virtualization is a process by which a virtual version of some actual thing is created. In computing, this may involve virtualization of an operating system, network resources, server, storage device or even a desktop.

Technically, we can refer to virtualization as a technique that permits the sharing of one instance of a physical resource or application among multiple users or groups.

The technique involves the assignment of a logical name to physical storage of a given resource or application and offering a pointer to the specific resource or application as is required.

The Concept behind Virtualization

The process of creating a virtual machine over an existing hardware and operating system, is referred to as Hardware virtualization.

Hardware virtualization creates an environment that is separated logically from the actual machine.

The machine on which the creation of a virtual machine occurs is referred to as the host machine. On the other hand, the created virtual machine is technically referred to as a guest machine.

Types of Virtualization

The following are the different types of virtualization:

- Server virtualization.
- Storage virtualization.

- Operating system virtualization.
- Hardware virtualization.

Server Virtualization

When virtual machine manager (VMM)-virtual machine software-is directly installed on the server, then the process is referred to as server virtualization.

Why Server Virtualization?

Server virtualization is essential because it is possible to subdivide a physical server into multiple servers on a demand basis, and also for load balancing.

Storage Virtualization

This is the process that involves the grouping of multiple physical storage devices in a network so that they appear like a single storage device. Software applications are also used for the implementation of storage virtualization.

Why storage virtualization?

This is crucial for recovery and back-up reasons.

Operating System Virtualization

In this case, the virtual machine software (VMM) is installed directly on the operating system of the host machine. Unlike hardware virtualization, VMM is not installed on the hardware.

Why operating system virtualization?

Operating system virtualization comes in handy when there is a need to test applications on a different operating system platform.

Hardware Virtualization

In hardware virtualization, the virtual machine software is installed directly on the hardware system.

The hypervisor is charged with the responsibility of controlling and monitoring the memory, processor, and hardware resources.

We can install a different operating systems on the system and use it to run a lot of other applications—after virtualization of the hardware system.

Why hardware virtualization?

Hardware virtualization is largely important for server platforms since the control of virtual machines is not as difficult as the control of a physical server.

How Virtualization Works in Cloud Computing

Virtualization is a greatly potent concept in cloud computing. Normally, in cloud computing, users need to share resources available in the clouds. For instance, applications and files are some of the sharable resources that may be stored in the clouds. With virtualization, users are provided with a platform that making sharing of such resources a practical experience.

The primary goal of virtualization is to offer applications with their standard versions to users in the clouds. When new application versions are released, users look up to the software developer for the new release. This is possible but may turn out to be quite a hectic affair if all users have to download the new version from a central server. To resolve that issue, virtualized servers and software can be maintained by third parties at a fee, but cloud users can efficiently access the new software releases.

In summary, virtualization primarily means running several operating systems on one machine that shares all hardware resources.

This technique is hugely helpful because it makes it possible to pool network resources, and share them with different users conveniently and at less cost.

Chapter 3: Computer Network Communication Technologies

How computers communicate in a network

Communication among different computers in a network takes place when data is transmitted from one machine to another.

The transmitting computer is referred to the sender (source). The machine to which data is transmitted is referred to as the receiver (destination).

For communication to take place, data is transmitted in the form of data packets. For data to get to the desired destination, data packets are assigned source and destination addresses. The source address identifies the sender. On the other hand, the destination address identifies the receiver (destination).

There are different ways in which data may be transmitted from one machine to another. Notably, there is more than one way in which data transmission happens.

The way in which data can be transmitted from one computer to another is referred to as data transmission mode. The transmission mode is also referred to as communication mode.

The different data transmission modes include the following:

- Simplex mode: communication goes on in one direction. That is, the communication is unidirectional. A device can only receive data but can't send, and vice-versa.
- Half-duplex mode: communication is bidirectional. That is, a device can send and receive data. However, it cannot send and receive at the same time.

- Full-duplex mode: communication is bidirectional. Unlike in half-duplex mode, communicating devices can transmit and receive at the same time.

Addressing

A message needs to originate from a known sender and be clearly addressed to a known recipient.

For instance, the traditional post office requires that the sender identifies himself or herself by name and location. The sender must also indicate the recipient's name and exact location (address).

Similarly, computers in a network are identified by their MAC addresses and IP addresses. MAC addresses are embedded on the computers' NICs while IP addresses are manually assigned during the configuration process, or the IP addresses are dynamically assigned by enabling the Dynamic Host Configuration Protocol (DHCP) on each machine. Each and every network host has a unique MAC address and unique IP address that identifies the given machine.

Understanding Ethernet

Ethernet network architecture is the most widespread of all network architecture all over the globe. We're going to examine the depths of this architecture and most likely find out why this architecture is as popular as it is.

Most network peripheral components have a built-in NIC. As a result, they can be easily plugged into an Ethernet wall outlet. It must be noted that the standard predetermined Ethernet length of wire of 100m from a hub or switch remains, so even when it comes to NIC-equipped print servers and printers, just as it is the case with workstations.

Printers that do not have a built-in NIC can still be used on a network by getting a connection with a network print server through a parallel, serial, or USB port or onboard NIC.

Ethernet Network Access Strategy

Suffice to say; Ethernet is a passive network architecture that embraces the wait-and-listen approach. It is also referred to as contention-based architecture since all computers on the network have to contend with the time of transmission on a given network medium.

Access to Ethernet networks is via CSMA/CD. This simply means that the network hosts have to listen to the network until the transmission medium is clear so that they can also transmit. Basically, they have to "sense" and determine that the line is indeed clear to initiate their own data transmission processes. A network host only sends out its data once it "feels" that the transmission is clear. In case there are multiple transmissions, a collision or collisions take place on the transmission medium. The machines sense the collisions and immediately halt their transmission processes.

One of the machines starts the retransmission as the others wait for the line to clear before they can retransmit their data. This process happens until the entire networks have completed their transmissions.

In a similar fashion, hosts wait and listen on the line for data meant for them. When a particular host senses that incoming is mean for them, they open the door for its reception and actually does receive the data onto its NIC interface. Ethernet is characterized by frequent collisions. As a result, some devices have a collision to prompt you when a collision happens. In fact, collisions are the main limitations of the Ethernet architecture. On the other hand, Ethernet is the most affordable of all other network architectures.

Note:

- Collisions slow down the network.
- Excess collisions may bring down a network completely.

Fast Ethernet

The traditional Ethernet has a speed of 10Mbps. Fast Ethernet offers a speed that is higher than the original 10Mbps. It has a 100Mbps transfer rate. The throughput is higher than the traditional Ethernet standard since the time it takes to transmit data over a network medium has been minimized by a whopping factor of 10. Thus, Fast Ethernet works at a rate that is 10 times the traditional speed of 10Mbps.

Traditionally, hubs and other connecting devices were designed to accommodate the 10 Mbps transfer rate. For such devices, Fast Ethernet is not supported. Fortunately, many connecting devices are being with NICs that can comfortably handle both 10Mbps and 100Mbps transfer rates. That means that the devices can accommodate both the original 10Mbps Ethernet as well the Fast Ethernet.

Gigabit Ethernet

This is another version of Ethernet that is even faster than Fast Ethernet. It uses the same data formats and IEEE Ethernet specifications a just like the other Ethernets-10Mbps and Fast Ethernet.

With Gigabit Ethernet, users are able to enjoy 1000Mbps transfer on a network. Unlike Fast Ethernet that operates on both twisted-pair cables and fiber-optic cables, Gigabit Ethernet was initially restricted to fiber—optic cabling. This required that a LAN be set up with specialized servers and high-speed switches. Gigabit Ethernet was considered to be a backbone for large LANs that required high transmission speeds.

Currently, anyone can practically enjoy the amazing high speeds of Gigabit Ethernet since it is being bundled out in network cards that can be conveniently installed in network servers and network clients.

Ethernet IEEE Cable Specifications

The following is a list showing some of the Ethernet specifications:

- 802.3 for Ethernet LAN.
- 802.5 for Token-Ring LAN.

- 802.7 for Broadband TAG.
- 802.8 for Fiber-Optic TAG.
- 802.9 for Data Networks and Integrated Voice.
- 802.10 for Network Security.
- 802.11 for Wireless Networks.

  Note: TAG stands for Technical Advisory Group.

The following points must be taken into account:

- Ethernet is well-defined by the IEEE specifications of 802.3.
- It works at the Data Link Layer of the OSI model.
- A number of the various IEEE types of Ethernet are available depending on the nature of cabling preferred on the given computer network.

These types of Ethernet-Gigabit Ethernet and Fast Ether-are designated by 3-part names, like 10BASE-T. The first section of the name describes the transmission speed. For instance, 10 specifies a 10Mbps Ethernet.

The second part of the name, which is "base" for all the different forms of Ethernet, indicates that the Ethernet signal is baseband. This means that the data drifts in a stream as one signal. This type of data transmission cannot allow the transmission of multiple channels of data or information as can the alternative-the broadband.

The last part of the Ethernet type name specifies the type of cable in use. For instance, in 10BASE-T, the T indicates a twisted-pair cable, and it is presumed to be an unshielded twisted-pair cable.

10BASE-T: This type of Ethernet works with a twisted-pair cable (unshielded twisted cable). The maximum cable length (without signal amplification) is 100m. 10BASE-T is operable on a star topology.

10BASE-2: This type of Ethernet works with a fairly flexible coaxial cable (RG-58A/U I or a thinnet), with a maximum cable length of 185m (this is rounded off to 200. Thus, the 2 in 10BASE-2). With the use of T-connectors to link the cabling to the network hosts' network cards, 10BASE-2 uses a bus topology. Though 10BASE-2 has always been the most pocket-friendly option for the Ethernet implementation, 10BASE-T setups are presently the most widespread.

10BASE-5: This is a type of Ethernet that uses a large-gauge coaxial cable (also referred to as thicknet), and the hosts on the network are linked to the main trunk line. The cables from the network host join the main trunk cable using vampire tabs, which pierce the primary trunk cable.

100BASE-TX: This is the type of Fast Ethernet that relies on the same Category 5 UTP cabling that is available on 10BASE-T Ethernet. This enactment can also employ 100-Ohm shielded twisted pair cable. The maximum cable length in the absence of a repeater is 100 meters.

100BASE-T4: This is the sort of Fast Ethernet that runs over Category 5 cabling, as can the 100BASE-TX. However, it can as well run over lower-grade twisted-pair cabling like Categories 3 and 4. In this type of Ethernet, the maximum cable run is the standard 100m length.

100BASE-FX: This is the sort of Fast Ethernet that spans over fiber-optic cable with a maximum length of 412m.

1000Base-T: This is the kind of Gigabit Ethernet that delivers 1000Mbps over Category 5 twisted pair cables.

10Gigabit Ethernet. This is the kind of Ethernet that delivers 10 billion bits per second over fiber optic cables.

Peer-to-Peer Communication

The peer-to-peer network setup offers a simple and cost-friendly networking solution in which the basic networking functions are needed. Peer-to-peer is ideal where file sharing and other basic resources such as printers. In this networking arrangement, there is no need for a dedicated server. The elimination of a network from the budget makes this kind of networking a highly pocket-friendly venture. It must be understood that network servers are quite expensive. They significantly contribute to the overall cost of a network. Therefore, its omission from the shopping list is a great way of cutting down on the installation cost of a network, as well as the overall management of the network. It is the ideal option for the implementation of small networks.

Features of Peer-to-Peer Networking

The following are the main features of Peer-to-Peer Networking:

- All network computers have equal privileges. They behave like peers.
- Each network host acts like both client and server. Essentially, a network can send out requests to other network hosts. Similarly, each host can receive requests from other any other hosts on the network.
- There is centralized administration of resources. This is due to the omission of a dedicated server from the setup. This also forms a concrete basis for connoting a peer-to-peer network as a workgroup. The peers collaborate freely without any centralized control or regulation.
- You only need to install an operating system on each peer and then physically connecting the peers via the NICs (NICs are not even necessary when working with Macintosh computers).

Merits of Peer-to-Peer Communication

The following are the main advantages of a peer-to-peer network implementation:

- Peer-to-peer network implementations are easy to install since they only involve the installation of operating systems on peer computers and physically connecting them.
- They are less expensive since a costly server computer is not needed. Furthermore, a Network Operating System (NOS) is also not needed.
- All required is readily available, most of which come packaged in your operating system.
- The network implementation is reliable since the failure or malfunction of a single peer does not lead to failure of another or failure of the entire network.

Demerits of Peer-to-Peer Communication

The following are the main limitations of a peer-to-peer network:

- If multiple users access a printer that is connected to your computer, your computer's processing resources are used as the printer serves your peers.

- There are challenges when it comes to data backups since there is no centralized location for sharable files.
- Resource management is difficult since resources have to be managed one by one.
- It is quite difficult to manage resources since resources are scattered all over the network.
- The security of the network might be easily compromised. Also, users might have to keep track of multiple network access credentials (usernames and passwords).

Chapter 4: The Internet

Internet basics

This section covers some of the basic technology concepts that make the Internet work and discuss various options for connecting to the information superhighway so that everyone on your network can surf the Internet, communicate via e-mail, share digital pictures with others, conduct research using countless online resources, make purchases online, download movies and music, video conference, and more.

Internet Technical Terms

Just as you don't necessarily need to know the inner works of a combustion engine to drive a car, it's not imperative that you understand every aspect of how the Internet works in order to take advantage of all that it offers. That said, it never hurts to examine, however briefly, the various terms and concepts that relate to the Internet.

TCP/IP

TCP/IP—short for Transmission Control Protocol/Internet Protocol—is a group of rules called protocols that define how devices, be they similar or diverse (i.e., computers, routers, and modems), connect and communicate with each other. (In this context, a "protocol" describes technical details about how any two communication devices will interact and work together to move digital data from one device to another).

TCP/IP works by determining the best available transmission path for data to travel. Rather than sending all the data in one large chunk, however, the protocol breaks the data into small packets.

These packets can travel over any number of different paths to reach their destination; when they arrive, they are reassembled in order.

To ensure that packets arrive at the correct destination, each one contains both the destination address and the source address. This information is stored in each packet's "envelope" or "header."

The TCP port of the protocol controls the breakdown of data on the sending end and its reassembly on the receiving end, while IP handles the routing of the data packets.

Think of it this way: Sending data via TCP/IP is not unlike sending letters via the U.S. Postal.

Service each letter you send by post contains the sender's address (i.e., the source address) and the recipient's address (i.e., the destination address). The difference is that with snail mail, you send the whole letter in one package or envelope (packet). If you were to send that same letter over the Internet, it would be sent in hundreds if not thousands of packets (envelopes) to get to its destination, after which it would be electronically reassembled.

Internet protocols in use under the TCP/IP banner include UDP, PPP, SLIP, VoIP, and FTP.

Subnet Mask

A su-net mask is a number applied within a host configuration file that allows for the division of an IP class C network into separately routable networks. For home networks on an ISP's larger network, the subnet mask will most often be 255.255.255.0, because home networks are not usually split into physically separate segments with internal routers. In-office buildings and business environments, subnets are used to detach traffic onto physically isolated networks to retain the data traffic on the low and to enhance performance for access to peripherals and local servers. Data traffic destined for another subnet or to the WAN will have to pass through the router.

DNS

Just as it is easier to remember someone's name than it is to remember her phone number, so, too, is it easier to remember the location of a Web site by its domain name rather than its IP address. For example, suppose you frequently visit the Web site of Ford Motor Company. Chances are, you will probably remember the site's domain name-i.e., Ford.com-and not its IP address. Your computer's Web browser, however, operates in the exact opposite way. It needs to know Ford.com's IP address in order to connect with the site.

That's the point domain name system comes in. When you enter the domain name of a site you want to visit (Ford.com), your Web browser initiates a session with a DNS server either locally or on the Internet to locate the IP address associated with that domain name. DNS servers perform a hierarchical lookup for the IP addresses using domain name associations for registered domain names to locate the IP address of the site you want to visit. If the DNS server your computer is linked to cannot determine the IP address linked with the domain name you entered, the DNS server will then look up the number on successively higher-level DNS servers until it finds the entry (or errors out).

Once the IP address is found, your computer can locate and communicate with the computer housing the Ford.com Web site. The first DNS server stores the association in memory for a time in case you or someone else it serves needs to visit that site again. The DNS server stores only frequently used associations because it can look up the ones it does not know on the higher-level DNS servers.

Assessing Internet Service Plans

Two things are necessary to establish home access to the Internet: at least one Internet-capable computer on your network and the purchase of an Internet service plan from an Internet service provider (ISP). What plans are available will vary somewhat by geography (with suburban and rural areas having fewer options than urban ones), the communication media you want to use, and the options put forth by your ISP.

Some critical plan features include the following:

- Price.
- Internet speed.
- Equipment provided by ISP.
- Customer service support.
- Nature of IP addresses provided-static or dynamic.
- Transmission media used.
- E-mail addresses.

- Webpage hosting.
- Complimentary Wi-Fi access.

Making the Connection

To connect your computer to the Internet, you must choose from the service-plan options available in your area. Once you have evaluated the connection plans and media options in your area, and have selected an ISP, review some of the following considerations below for guidelines on how to set up Internet access.

Connecting with Dial-Up

Dial-up is, for the most part, obsolete from a speed perspective, but in some rural areas, it is the only available low-cost Internet-connection option. When connecting your computer using dial-up over a plain old telephone service (POTS) line, there are three common scenarios:

- Hooking up a computer or laptop with a built-in modem.
- Using an external dial-up modem connected via a USB port.

- Using a modem that will connect to a 9-pin serial port.

Connecting with Cable

A popular Internet-connection choice in many areas is cable. In fact, your home or small office may already have a cable connection for television service, making the addition of a cable modem to the mix fairly simple. Cable Internet service is high speed-much better than that offered by dial-up. In addition, many cable-based packages bundle increased television channels for viewing and Internet phone service.

Connecting with Wireless (Wi-Fi)

Connecting wirelessly to the Internet is fairly simple, but your network must include a gateway or router designed for wireless connections. In addition, any computers on your network must have Wi-Fi capabilities built-in or, in the case of a laptop or notebook computer, a slot for a wireless Wi-Fi card.

If your computer or workstations are not configured for Wi-Fi, fear not. There are hosts of manufacturers making devices to support wireless connections—essentially, these are portable wireless NICs that can be plugged into either an Ethernet port or a USB port.

Connecting with DSL

Using DSL to connect to the Internet over standard phone lines has an advantage of accessing the internets are higher speeds than the dial-up option (assuming you live in an area where DSL service is available). Moreover, whereas a dial-up connection relies upon the audio/analog band on a phone line, data on a DSL Internet connection passes over the wire pair at a frequency that is higher-meaning that users can still use their phone lines while at the same time using the Internet (and, by extension, keep your Internet connection live 24/7).

Network Address Translation

Network address translation (NAT) is an important feature on Internet-connected devices and gateways that allows a computer to have an IP address that is not visible on the Internet, yet still, receive and send data packets over the Internet. These addresses are hidden and are assigned from a different set of IP addresses-called private IP addresses-from the addresses that are seen or exposed on the Internet. These private addresses are assigned to computers inside the firewall, enabling them to use TCP/IP protocols for communicating to internal devices and to hosts on the Internet without being seen-thereby, making it harder to hack into the internal computer. Using NAT is the first tier in firewalling or protecting your network computers from unwanted intruders anywhere on the Internet.

Private IP addresses also extend the connectivity of the Internet to more computers than there are available IP addresses because the same private, internal network IP address can be used at hundreds, thousands, or even millions of locations.

It works like this: When you open a browser to reach, for example, Yahoo.com, the data packet reaches your Internet gateway/firewall, which in turn starts a session to keep track of your MAC address and IP address. It then replaces your private IP address from the data packet with its own visible IP address in the data packet and sends the request to Yahoo.com. When the information is returned from Yahoo for your session, the process is reversed; the Internet gateway/firewall strips out its own IP address, re-inserts your computer's private IP address and MAC address into the packet header and passes the packet down the network wire to your computer.

When this happens, your internal IP address is said to have been "network address translated"-although a better term might be "network address substituted." By default, most home network gateways use NAT and assign private IP addresses to all the computers on the home network.

Private Networks

Private networks are IP networks with host computers that hide behind a device that provides NAT. The computers on these networks are assigned IP addresses outside of the pool of numbers used on the Internet. Essentially, any number in the private address range can be assigned locally to a computer or host.

Private network IP addresses begin with any of the following numbers:

- 10
- 172.16–172.31
- 192.168

A complete example might be 192.168.11.4 or 10.101.101.1.

Worldwide Web: Window to the World

Like a living organism, the Web is constantly changing as networks are added or changed. The growth of the Internet both in geographic reach and audience presents every connected entity with opportunities to communicate like never before in history. If your use of the Web is limited to simply downloading information and receiving e-mail, you are hardly scratching the surface of what can be accomplished over the Web. Ways to use the Web to inform, educate, and exchange ideas, goods, and services with a worldwide audience are limited only by one's imagination and creativity. This chapter merely skims the surface of what you can do on the Web.

Leveraging Your Connection to the Web

Connecting your network-or a sub-network of your network-to the Internet stretches the reach of your home or office network to the far corners of the earth.

For under $120 per month in most markets around the country, you can obtain a connection to the Internet that runs at decent speeds and includes up to five static IP addresses.

These addresses can significantly enhance your ability to garner the most benefit from your connection to the Internet. That's because, in order to make Web servers, Webcams, and other resources available on the Web, you need at least one static IP address that is visible on the Internet. Additionally, a static IP address can be used to enable VPN clients to connect to your network resources. Without a static IP address, much of your communication to the outside world is limited. With a static IP address, however, your network can become a Web site, client-services provider, radio station, TV station, or blog-just, to name a few.

The Web really is a window on the world. Not only can you see out, obtaining incredible amounts of data from the Web, so too can others anywhere in the world see in, enabling you to share information of your choosing with a worldwide audience. Adding your own resources to the Web-the ultimate unfettered two-way, free-speech forum-can both provide value to you and your organization and increase the utility of the Web for others.

Popular Uses of the Web

The following are the main uses of the web:

Finding or Publishing Information

Most people use the Internet to obtain information-which is why some people call it the largest library in the world. The best way to obtain information online is to enter keywords or phrases into a search engine like Yahoo, Google, and Ask.

When you type a keyword or phrase into the search field on any one of these sites, it returns any number of links to Web pages that relate to the word or phrase you entered. Ask yourself or your organization's management: What information about you, your family, or your company should be posted to a Web server?

There is more to getting your information found or your voice heard on the Internet than simply getting a domain name such as thisismywebsite.com. To ensure that the information on your site can be found when someone performs a related search, you enter key search words into your document headings and possibly pay to register your site with various search engines. Learning key search words and adapting your document headings and labels accordingly is a science in itself. And even if you master it, your business Web site might be listed at the top of the search results one day and slip to 100 or 1,000 the next. Like the Wild West, there are few rules on the Internet and anything goes when it comes to getting noticed.

Communication

This takes place in the following ways:

E-mail

The most popular Internet communication tool is e-mail- that is, messages are sent electronically from sender to host on the Internet, potentially forwarded to other hosts, and ultimately downloaded at the recipient's convenience.

One way to obtain an e-mail account is from your Internet service provider (ISP); most plans include the use of at least one e-mail address. Alternatively, you might run your own home or office e-mail server under a domain name you own. You access messages received via these accounts through special software called an e-mail client.

Another option is to use any one of several free Web browsers–accessible e-mail services, such as the following:

- Yahoo! Mail (http://mail.yahoo.com).
- Gmail (http://www.gmail.com).

Instant Messaging (IM)

Another way to communicate over the Internet is via instant messaging (IM). IM provides instant communication; there is no middleman to store or forward the message. Both end-users must be online to IM; when they do, the text they type is transmitted instantly from one to the other in back-and-forth fashion the second the Send button (or similar) is clicked. You can IM using an IM client on your desktop or, in some cases, a Web browser. Popular instant-messaging applications include the following:

- Yahoo! Messenger.
- Window Live Messenger.

Video Conferencing

Video conferencing gives users the rare chance of conducting virtual meetings, thereby saving on a lot of travel expenses. To do a video conference over the Internet, at least one participant ought to have a static IP address visible to the Internet. Additionally, each participant should have service with an upload speed of at least 400Kbps to maintain quality communications, particularly if you're using the video component. To video conference, you must have access to a Webcam of some sort.

Blogging

Blogs, short for Weblogs, are sites on which people can share information with other interested or likeminded individuals. Think of a blog as a digital journal that can be read by people around the world.

Entertainment and Media

The Internet boasts a plethora of entertainment options, including the following:

- Interactive gaming.
- Music.
- Video.
- News.
- Internet radio.

- Internet television.

Engaging in Commerce

Commerce represents one of the most common uses of the Internet. Business-related activities include (but are not limited to) the following:

- Banking.
- Advertising.
- Retail sales and marketing.
- Auctions.

Downloading Software

Much major software publishers-including Microsoft, Corel, and Sun-offer users the ability to download what would otherwise be boxed commercial off-the-shelf software (COTS). All you need is a good Internet connection and a PayPal account, credit card, or in some cases, a checkbook to pay the fee. There is also a wide variety of trial software, freeware, and shareware, as well as open-source software, available for download online.

Surveillance

Setting up surveillance cameras to be viewed over the Web is nearly a plug-and-play operation, provided you have the necessary IP addresses to support the camera or Web servers. This technology allows, for example, monitoring of your home or office while away or, say, checking on your summer house while you are at home.

Business owners can set up cameras at their place of work to monitor events at the office or keep tabs while away.

Chapter 5: Router and Server Basics

Routers and servers are very important network devices. This section seeks to outline some of the fundamental concepts of routing as well as the client/server architecture. We're also going to examine a VLAN and how to configure it.

Router: what is it, and what does it do?

A router is just another networking device that primarily connects different networks. A router plays the role of forwarding data packets based on what information is contained in the header of a data packet.

This is a device that operates in the network layer of the OSI model. In the TCP/IP model, a router operates in the internet layer.

Routing refers to the process of determining the best path along which data transmission takes place-from source to destination. Routing is done by a router, which has been defined above.

Routing algorithms are responsible for actualizing the routing process. The routing algorithms refer to a piece of software that works behind the scenes to ensure that the most appropriate path is selected for the transmission of data from sender to receiver.

The routing algorithms are also responsible for the initialization of the routing table. They are also responsible for the maintenance of the routing table.

Routing metrics are used by routing protocols in the determination of the best path for data transmission. Routing metrics include hop count, delay, bandwidth, and current load among others.

Routing Metrics and Costs

Metrics and costs play a key role in determining the best path. Metrics refer to network variables that are considered in the determination of the best path. Routing metrics include the following:

- Delay: this refers to the time that a router takes in the queuing, processing, and transmitting of data to a given interface. The path with the lowest delay value is unquestionably taken to be the best path.
- Hop Count: this refers to a metric that offers a specification of passes through a connecting device

like a router. The path with the lowest hop count is preferred to any other available path if routing protocols consider the hop as a primary variable.

- Bandwidth: this refers to the link capacity. It is given in bits per second. The transfer rates of all links are compared. The link with the highest transfer rate is embraced as the best path.
- Reliability: the reliability value is determined dynamically. Some links are more vulnerable to malfunctioning than others. Besides, some links are more easily repaired than others-after a breakdown. Whatever the case, a more reliable link is preferred to a less reliable link. The system administrator is charged with the responsibility of assigning reliability values, which are numeric in nature.
- Load: this is the degree of how busy a network link is at any given moment. It may be in the form of packets that are processed per unit time, processor utilization or memory use. The load increases with increasing traffic. In routing, the link with a lighter load is considered to be the best path for data transmission.

Routing Types

Routing appears in the following classifications:

Static Routing

This is also referred to as non-adaptive routing. The administrator has to add routes in the routing table manually. Packets are sent from source to destination along a path that's defined by the administrator. Routing does not depend on network topology or network state. It is the job of the administrator to decide the routes along which data are transmitted from source to destination.

Merits of static routing

- There is no overhead on router CPU usage.
- There is more security since the administrator has control over a particular network only.
- There is no bandwidth usage between different routers.

Limitations of Static Routing

- It is quite exhausting to come up with a routing table for a big network.

- The administrator must be highly knowledgeable in networking, and particularly in the network topology he or she's dealing with.

Default Routing

In this technique, router configuration is done in a way that a router sends all data packets to a single hop. It does not matter the network on which the hop is found. Packets are simply relayed to the machine on which it configured by default.

This technique is most ideal when a given network has to handle a single exit point. However, a router would choose another path that is specified in a routing table and ignore the one that's set by default.

Dynamic Routing

This is also referred to as adaptive routing. In this approach, a router determines the routing path as per the prevailing condition in the network.

Dynamic protocols, the heavy lifting when it comes to discovering new routes. These protocols are RIP and OSPF. Automatic adjustments are meant when particular routes fail to function as expected.

Features of Dynamic Protocols

The following are features of dynamic protocols:

- Routers must have the same protocols to exchange routes.
- A router broadcasts information to all connected routers in whenever it discovers an issue or issues in the topology or network status.

Merits of Dynamic Routing

- They're quite easy to configure.
- The best option when it comes determining the best paths due to changes in network status and topology.

Limits of Dynamic Routing

- It's a lot more costly when it comes to bandwidth and CPU usage.
- It's not as secure as default and static routing.

Important Notes!

- A router filters out network traffic not merely by packet address, but by a specific protocol.

- A router does not divide a network physically. It does so logically.
- IP routers divide networks into a number of subnets to ensure that specific network traffic meant for a particular IP address can be allowed to pass between specified network segments. However, this intelligent data forwarding leads to decreased speeds.
- Network efficiency is higher with the use of routers in complex networks.

Network Servers

A network server refers to a software application that runs a remote network machine to offer services to other machines on a given network.

Client computers in a network make requests to the server whenever they need certain services. The offers an open window for the client request but does not, at a given moment, initiate a service.

Servers are infinite programs that, when started, runs infinitely unless an issue pops up. A server always stands in wait for requests from client machines on a given network. The server responds appropriately to all incoming client requests.

Some networks do not have a dedicated server to control communication on the network. Given such arrangements, network devices communicate directly with one another. There are, however, a number of merits as well as demerits of servers in network operation.

Merits of Servers

The following are pros of using a server to handle client request on networks:

- Centralized administration ensures more security in respect of resource sharing.
- The use of a server provides a centralized back-up system since important data is stored in a server computer.
- There is increased network speed in respect of resource sharing.
- There is a higher scalability level since it's possible to expand the network in terms of clients and servers separately.

Limitations of Using Servers

- Traffic congestion is always a big issue when many clients have to send requests simultaneously.
- There is no robustness in a network since a breakdown or malfunction of a server derails all request handling features of a network.
- Specific hardware may be required at the server-side since a client/server network is greatly decisive.
- There may exist a resource on the server computer, but not on a client computer.

Servers are available in different forms. The following is a list of different servers that play highly significant roles in computer networks:

Access Servers

Remote (LAN) access offers network connectivity to remote users who may be otherwise constrained by geographic limitations of a LAN. An access server makes use of a telephone line to connect an office or user with an office network.

Network Time Servers

Network time servers are servers that handle all network timing information from different sources a including radio broadcasts and satellites. These servers then avail the gathered information (from different sources) to the given network.

Time servers rely of NTP and UDP/Time protocols to communicate with other nodes. In so doing, there is proper synchronization of coordinated activities in the network.

Device Servers

A device server refers to a specialized and network-based network device that meant to perform one or more server functions. A device has three main features that include client access and minimal operating architecture.

There is no per-seat operating system license in the minimal operating architecture. Also, client access is independent of any proprietary protocol or operating system.

Besides the above two features, a device server is a "closed-box" server. This means that it requires minimal maintenance, is easy to install, and is remotely manageable via a browser.

Examples of devices include network time servers, terminal servers, and print servers. These device servers are designed to handle perform specific tasks. Each device server is characterized by a unique set of configuration features in software and hardware. The unique features help these servers to work optimally.

Multiport Device Servers

These servers allow sharing of devices between terminals and hosts locally and all over a given network. One terminal can be connected to multiple hosts and can conveniently switch among the different hosts. Multiport device servers can as well be used on devices that have serial ports only.

A multiport device server can convert between known protocols such as TCP/IP and LAT. This is possible primarily due to a multiport device server's natural ability of translation.

Print Servers

The print servers make it possible for different network users to share network printers. A print server may support either a serial or parallel interface. As a result, the print server accepts requests from all network users using appropriate protocols. A print server also manages printing jobs on every network printer.

Understanding VLAN

VLAN is an acronym for Virtual Local Area Network (normally referred to as Virtual LAN). It refers to a switched network that is segmented logically using a project team, application, or function. The logical segmentation is done without consideration of users' physical locations.

VLANs are more or less the same as physical LANs. The only difference is that VLANs allow end stations to be grouped regardless of whether they are on the same physical segment or not.

A VLAN can accommodate any form of switch module port. Multicast, broadcast, and unicast data packets can be forwarded and flooded to end stations only in a given VLAN.

Each VLAN is taken as a logical network. Packets destined for stations outside of a VLAN must be forwarded through a router to reach its destination. Notably, a VLAN can be associated with an IP subnets.

Supported VLANs

Conventionally, we identify VLANs with a number ranging from 1 to 4094.

The following must be noted:

- 1002-1005 VLAN IDs are reserved for FDDI and Token Ring VLANs
- VLAN IDs > 1005 are not found in the VLAN database since they are extended range.
- Switch module supports extended-range and normal-range VLANs (1005).
- A number of configured features, SVIs, and routed ports affects the functioning of the switch module hardware.

VLAN Configuration Guidelines

It is important to understand the following facts:

- 1005 VLANs are supported on the switch module.
- Numbers between 1 and 1001 are used to identify normal-range VLANs.

- 1002 -1005 are reserved for FDDI and Token Ring VLANs.
- Switch module has no FDDI and Token Ring support.
- 1-1005 VLAN IDs are normally stored in the VLAN database, as well as the file containing the switch module configuration information.
- 1006-4094 (extended-range) VLAN IDs are limited to private LAN, RSPAN VLAN, MTU, and UNI-ENI VLANs. These VLAN IDs are not saved in the VLAN database.

The following steps will help you create or modify a VLAN:

1. Use the [**configure terminal**] command to enter the global configuration mode.
2. Enter the [**vlan <vlan-id>**] to enter VLAN configuration mode.

   -Use an existing VLAN ID to modify an existing VLAN.

   -Choose a new ID to create a new VLAN.

3. Use the command [**name <vlan-name>**] to give your VLAN a name.

   Though, this is optional for normal-range VLANs.

4. Use the [**mtu <mtu-size**>] to set the MTU size.

   This also optional.

5. Use the command [**end**] to return to privileged EXEC mode.

6. Use the [**show vlan {name vlan-name | id vlan-id}**].

7. Use the [**copy running-config startup config**] command to verify entries.

8. To delete a VLAN, use the command [**no vlan vlan-id**].

Note that VLAN 1 and VLANs 1002-1005 cannot be deleted.

Chapter 6: IP Addressing and IP sub-netting

IP Address

What is an IP address?

An Internet protocol (IP) address is a four-octet, eight-bit digital address (32 bits total) that, when written out, looks like this: 10.156.158.12. Evidently, an IP is a unique set of numbers that are separated by dots. The set of numbers is used to identify a computer (or network device) using Internet Protocol (IP) for network communication. In an IP address, the value of any of the octets—the numbers between the periods—can be from 0 to 255.

An IP address is not entirely different from a phone number. If you know someone's phone number—say, your Uncle Mike—you can call her by dialing her number on your telephone's keypad. Then, your phone company's computers and switching equipment go to work to connect your phone with the phone belonging to Uncle Mike over an audio communication channel.

Once connected, you can speak with buddy Bradley, even if he is many miles away. When you do, the audio signal carrying your voice will typically travel over a pair of copper wires from your house to a switch at your local phone company.

From there, the signal might be converted to a light wave in order to travel over a fiber optic cable to another switch. From this second switch, the audio signal might be converted to a radio-wave signal in order to travel from one microwave tower to another. Eventually, as the signal nears its destination-Uncle, Mike's house-it will be converted back to an analog audio signal, traveling over a pair of copper wires from Uncle Mike's phone company to her house. (This scenario assumes the use of landlines. If cell phones are involved, then this process will vary in the details, but not in the concept).

What is the Function of an IP Address?

In a similar fashion to how phones use numbers to connect on a local, regional, national, or international scale, an IP address facilitates connections between computer hosts as well as routing equipment. Put another way, if two computers on the Internet have each other's IP addresses, they can communicate. But unlike phones, which use switching equipment to connect, computers connect to each other over the Internet through the use of routing equipment, which shares the communication paths with hundreds or thousands of other computers.

When data is sent from a computer to a router, the router's job is to find a short, open communication path to another router that is both close to and connected to the destination computer.

The router accomplishes this either by using default routes or by dynamically learning and recording tables, called "routing tables," that keep track of which IP addresses are present on any one of the router's many open, up-and-running communication ports. Because all the routers connected together on the Internet resemble a spider's web, data can travel over many different routes or paths if necessary, to get to its intended destination. If one of the routers or some other connecting link goes offline, the other routers are trying to move the data search for an alternative route to the destination.

In order to facilitate this dynamic communication method, routers are also assigned IP addresses so they can find each other.

IP Sub-netting

Routed IP environments require that your pool of IP addresses be sub-netted. This allows each subnet to see itself as a separate segment of the larger internetwork. The router then ties together the various subnets into one network. The router knows how to route traffic to the correct segment because it builds a routing table. The routing table is basically the networks' roadmap.

IP sub-netting is fairly complex, and so to make this discussion informative but still digestible at an introductory level, we will limit our exploration of sub-netting to one class of IP addresses; we will look at an example of sub-netting a Class B range of IP addresses.

The mathematical tricks that we use to subnet the Class B network can also be used to sub-net a Class A or Class C network (although sub-netting Class C networks greatly limit the number of usable IP addressed that you end up with).

Sub-netting is a two-part process. First, you must determine the subnet mask for the network (it will be different than the default subnet masks; for example, the default for Class B is 255.255.0.0). After figuring out the new subnet mask for the network, you must then compute the range of IP addresses that will be in each sub-net.

Okay, let's cheat a little before we do the math of sub-netting a Class B network. I think it will aid in the overall understanding of the sub-netting process. The following table shows the new subnet masks, the number of subnets, and the number of hosts per subnet that would be creating when using a certain number of bits for sub-netting (the Bits Used column).

IPv4 vs. IPv6

Currently, IP version 4 (IPv4) addresses are the Internet IP addresses of choice. As mentioned, these addresses are composed of four sets of eight bits. In the future, we will likely adopt the IP version 6 (IPv6) address scheme. IPv6 differs in form and substance from IPv4 in two ways:

- IPv6 addresses have eight 16-bit numbers (128 bits total), usually expressed in four-digit hexadecimal form. The range of a single 16-bit number is greater than that of an eight-bit number, spanning from zero to 65,535.
- The 16-bit numbers in an IPv6 address are separated by colons rather than periods.

Why make the switch? Because under IPv4, there are not enough numbers available to assign one to every computer or device on the Internet that needs one. IPv6 solves this problem, offering 2 raised to the 128th power addresses; in contrast, IPv6 offers only 2 raised to the 32nd power-although masking, and private-address strategies have been used to extend the number of available IPv4 addresses on the Internet.

Chapter 7: Introduction to Cisco System and CCNA Certification

What is CCNA?

CCNA stands for Cisco Certified Network Associate. It is a widely held certification among computer network enthusiasts. This certification is valid for any computer network engineer that starts with the low-level network engineers, network support engineers, and network administrators through to network specialists.

The certification program was founded in 1998. An estimated 1 million certificates have been awarded to qualified persons ever since.

CCNA program spans numerous crucial networking concepts. It is an essential foundational course for interested candidates in preparation for current and emerging networking technologies.

CCNA Scope

The following are the major topics that feature greatly in CCNA certification program:

- Networking essentials-which include definition of network; description of network components, and the basic network setup and configuration requirements.
- IP addressing.
- The OSI Reference Model.
- IP Routing.
- Routers-routing protocols (OSPF, EIGRP and RIP).
- WLAN and VLAN.
- Network device security.

- Network security and management.
- Network troubleshooting.

Why CCNA?

- The CCNA certificate is a trusted validation of a networking professional's ability to manage and administer a routed and medium-level network. It is the validation of an individual's understands of a network and their ability to operate and configure it. It also certifies a person's ability to troubleshoot the network.
- The course offers lessons on how to meet network users' requirements by proper determination of network topology.
- Candidates learn how to make a point-point network.
- Protocol routing for connecting networks is also realized through CCNA certification.
- Network address construction is adequately explained in the CCNA certification course.

- The course offers a comprehensive explanation on the establishment of a connection with a remote network.
- CCNA certification is offered using easy-to-understand study material.
- The course is a prerequisite for other important CISCO certification programs such as CCNA Wireless, CCNA Security and CCNA Voice, among others.
- CCNA certification program equips learners with the necessary knowledge and skills for the installation, configuration, and management of a small LAN and WAN service networks.

Different Forms of CCNA Certifications

There are two main approaches to fulfilling a CCNA certification course:

1. Combined CCNA Exam.
2. ICND1 Exam and ICND2.

Note that every CCNA certificate is only valid for a period of 3 years. Every holder of a CCNA certificate is expected to take a fresh examination after every 3 years.

Chapter 8: Fundamentals of Network Security

Network security is one of the most important aspects of the overall computer. Now, more than ever, having an adequate security protocol that can combine both functionality and protection is essential for all types of users.

Amid a large number of threats out there, users must have a system that they can rely on when going about their usual day to day business. In that regard, the need to integrate these aspects motivates users to find the ideal solution to their individual needs.

In this chapter, we are going to be taking a look at the fundamentals of network security, guidelines, and best practices, as well as the most common threats, found lurking today. In addition, we are going to be discussing the ways in which the average user can take better care to avoid becoming the victim of unscrupulous folks out there.

The Only Thing to Panic Is Fear Itself

It's natural for the average user to fear hackers. This may lead the average user to spend a pretty penny on security measures, which may or may not offer the combination of security and functionality that such users need. In fact, the most common side effect of top-notch security measures is a slow system. For example, a solid online security system will essentially scan every single bit of information that goes through their system. However, this can lead to an overall slowing of internet connection speeds.

As a result, users may feel that they have been short-changed by the performance of their security system. Other systems may sacrifice certain safety features in exchange for faster performance and internet speeds. Yet, these tradeoffs may leave critical information and transactions vulnerable to unwanted folks.

That is why the first thing to keep in mind is that breaking the bank out of fear of being vulnerable may lead you to overspend on a system that, while keeping your system safe, may end up costing you more in the end. That is why finding the right balance is essential; striking a balance between features and performance is the ultimate goal of all users. Therefore, we will be taking an objective look at what threats are out there, which ones you will most likely be vulnerable to, and what you can do to protect yourself.

Please keep one thing in mind: of all the horror stories out there, some may not necessarily apply to so long as you don't engage in the types of practices that attract hackers and fraudsters, such as handle a large volume of financial transactions on a daily basis. Consequently, taking the proper steps to secure the transactions that you do make will go a long way toward keeping your information and your money safe.

What to Be on the Lookout For

Threats are out there, and they are real. However, the most important thing to keep in mind is that hackers and fraudsters love feeding on low-hanging fruit.

What does that mean?

It means that cheaters are looking for vulnerable people who don't know any better. Hence, they prey on these individuals. This is why the elderly are a common target for phone scammers. As such, online cheaters are looking for folks, who have left windows unlocked or have neglected to ensure their information is safe.

Also, please keep in mind that a lot of the fraudsters and hackers out there will essentially go on a phishing expedition. That's right, we mean "phishing" and not "fishing" since hackers tend to cast a wide net in search of unsuspecting victims.

As a matter of fact, phishing is one of the most common means of victimizing individuals. A hacker will go the extra mile to produce an official-looking e-mail in which they feign to be part of some organization, such as a bank, in which you are registered. Now, they have no way of knowing if you are actually a customer of that bank. So, the e-mail needs to look as natural as possible so that, in the event that you are actually a customer of that bank, you will believe that it is an official communication. The scammers then trick the user into providing their username and password under the pretense that the bank is undergoing security updates, and so on. When the unsuspecting victim falls for the scam, it is quite plausible that the crooks will then proceed to empty the victim's bank account.

This scam was so predominant that virtually every company out there took the necessary steps to ensure that their customers would not be subject to these attacks. In the end, phishing has been essentially crushed. Nevertheless, there are one, or two, hackers out there who still give it the old college try.

That being said, the following threats outlined in this chapter are examples of what you need to be on the lookout for.

Network Intruders

Intruders are lurking about. There is no doubt about that. It should be noted that most intrusion events happen from within. That means that intruders are generally people who have access to the network and seek to gain unauthorized access to other parts of the network.

Thus, it is important to have a clear picture of who has access to what and how sensitive information ought to be protected. For instance, if a company handles personal information belonging to their customers, great care needs to be taken in order to ensure that such information does not fall into the wrong hands. This is especially critical if such information could potentially become profitable.

A good practice in this regard is to update the roster of individuals who have access to your network, or your personal computer for that matter. That way, if a breach should happen to occur, it will be easier to pinpoint who has access to what and where the breach may have originated.

Outside intruders may attempt some kind of remote access to your network, but they would at least need to have some kind of insight into usernames and passwords. Although, it's worth pointing out that hackers need only a healthy list of usernames because, as we will see in a moment, they can use other means to break through a password.

Social Engineering

Phishing is an example of social engineering. As such, social engineering seeks to use clever tactics in order to extract as much information as possible from potential victims. That is why all users need to take care with sensitive information in all means of online interaction. For example, hackers may be circling the water on social media, looking for unsuspecting prey to pounce on. If you are getting visions of sharks swimming about, then you are right on the money. The fact of the matter is that hackers will often pose as customer service agents pretending to help customers regain access to their accounts or open a new one. Even if the customer does not reveal all of their information, the hacker may get just enough to breach an account.

The saying, "if it's too good to be true, it probably is" still rings true when it comes to social engineering. So, always keep an eye out for any suspicious activity out there. If you are even in doubt, just stay away from suspicious users and websites.

Password hacking

Virtually every type of network requires two things to access it: a username and a password. Even if hackers happen to get their hands on your username, they still have to crack your password. This can be rather complex. Yet, you can make it easy for hackers if you don't pay close attention to the types of passwords you are using.

Currently, most sites and network protocols require passwords to have a combination of letters, numbers, and special characters (@, #, & or *). In short, the longer your password is the better. In fact, the best passwords make use of random characters and numbers. This makes it virtually impossible for password cracking software to get its hands on your password.

For instance, "happy" isn't exactly the safest password. It may take a password cracking software minutes to break it. However, a password like "H@ppy" is far more complex and may take password cracking software days to or even weeks before it is able to get anywhere. By then, the hacker will have given up and moved on to the next target.

If you happen to use a password generator software, please bear in mind that you will get a password of around 16 characters using random letters numbers and special characters. Perhaps the best piece of advice here is to make sure that your passwords don't have any type of logical connection to you. They need to be as random as possible. That way, you can ensure that your account will be as safe as it can be.

Packet sniffing

This is a complex endeavor, but if successful, a hacker can have access to potentially unlimited amounts of data. This requires the hacker to install software that can read the information traffic going through your network. If your information is not encrypted, then you are just a sitting duck. That is why most network routers come with their own built-in encryption. Furthermore, free webmail services also use their own encryption. That way, if a hacker happens to intercept your package, the only thing they will be able to get is meaningless gibberish. It may end up taking the week or months before they are able to even get close to breaking through the encryption. While it is not impossible, it will certainly deter hackers from wasting their time on your data.

Exploiting vulnerabilities

Nothing is perfect, and software is no exception. That is why the shark metaphor is so apt when it comes to hackers. They are consistently circling the water looking for backdoors, loopholes, and other coding errors that may allow then access to a network. In fact, an entire industry has been built around hacking large corporations and then extorting them out of large sums of money. If the software you are using happens to have one such mistake, you might be vulnerable to an intrusion. These issues are generally addressed by software manufacturers and solved as promptly as possible. However, software manufacturers don't generally become aware of the problem until someone's network has been breached. Nevertheless, always be on the lookout for software updates and security patches. That way, you can improve the overall level of protection in your network.

Malware

This has got to be the most common means of granting unauthorized access to wrongdoers. Malware consists of a program that latches onto your computer files and opens a door for hackers to walk through. When installed, it may be very difficult to detect its presence. Most of the time, you will pick up on it until it's too late. The most common form of malware is a program commonly referred to as a virus.

Now, malware is completely ineffective unless one thing happens: the user needs to allow the malware package to enter their computer. This can be done through a download, inserting a pen drive or installing software.

Often, malware poses as another type of software, thereby tricking the user into opening the file, installing the program, or downloading the virus. In such cases, you can still kill the program from ruining your computer though you would have to kill it immediately. A good antivirus program will help keep you safe, especially if you usually download information online.

The best thing you can do to protect yourself, in this case, is to avoid opening any e-mail attachments, downloading software, or installing anything that isn't from a trusted source or that might look fishy.

Denial of Service (Ransomware)

Ransomware works in the same manner as malware does but with one particular twist: malware generally looks to snoop on your activity and steal information such as account numbers, passwords and usernames, whereas ransomware will lock up your computer and deny you access to your network. What the hackers are after in this case is a payment in order to liberate your system and/or files. However, once you pay, there is no guarantee they won't try it again. If you should ever fall prey to a ransomware attack, you need to drastically overhaul your security settings. Otherwise, it will only be a matter of time before hackers try the same shenanigans again.

What can be done about these threats?

Fortunately, there is plenty that can be done to ensure the security of your network. We have already pointed out some of the best practices which you can implement as a part of your usual activity. Moreover, there are other measures which you can take so that you can avoid becoming a target of unwanted attacks.

Network Security Areas or Zones

In a perfect world, there would be a single solution to all of the threats we have outlined. However, engineers are yet to produce a one-size-fits-all solution. The main reason for this is that hackers like keeping up with the times; that is, as soon as security measured is implemented, hackers are looking for a workaround.

That being said, let's take a look at the various network areas, or zones, which comprise a typical network apparatus.

Logical Security Zones

The most common type of network is a small, home-based network. Typically, these networks consist of internet access coming from an ISP into a router installed in a customer's home. Then, various devices are connected to this network in order to access the internet.

Now, in general terms, most home networks are relatively safe given the type of security measures that come preinstalled with the equipment that the average user purchases. Unless users attempt to access the dark web or frequently download software from untrusted sources, then the risks should be minimal.

There are two types of traffic that you will find in this type of setup, intranet traffic, and internet traffic. Intranet traffic is all of the traffic that happens within the network itself. This traffic cannot be accessed by anyone that does not have access to the network. Unless the network is somehow compromised, the data contained within is rather bulletproof.

Internet traffic is any data that comes in or goes out of the network. This is where things get tricky. If care is not taken to encrypt data or restrict access, then the network may be compromised. One simple example of compromise could be removing your router's password, thereby leaving it as an open network. That means that anyone can access your network and even play with your router. This could lead to packet sniffing and interception of your data.

Therefore, great care needs to be taken to restrict access to wireless data points. If you are not careful to restrict network access through the use of a username and password, you would be opening up the door to unwanted intruders.

Data security areas or zones

The next level of security is protecting the data itself. So, even if the network is comprised and subsequently breached by an unwanted intruder, the data package will be useless to them unless they are able to break the encryption. High-level encryption is virtually impossible to break. This can only be done through the use of the algorithm, which was used to encrypt the data in the first place. So, unless the hacker actually has access to the algorithm, there is not much they can do to break it.

It should be noted that if the data is encrypted with a low-level algorithm, then there is a chance that a very clever hacker could break the code and subsequently crack into your data. However, sites and networks that use 128-bit encryption are essentially bulletproof as cracking through encryption that complex may take forever. Unless a hacker is somehow unusually determined to break through, they will give up when they see that breaking through may take them years to achieve.

Physical Access areas or zones

This is the next line of network security. It is also arguably the most important since a breach in the physical security of a network can lead to catastrophic results. This is the reason why you see armed guards at the door of server rooms, or at the entrance of building physical housing equipment.

While physical security doesn't always need to go to such extremes, it is important to protect access to physical equipment. Often, the biggest breaches of security don't occur as a result of a hack, but rather, they are the work of an individual who gains access to physical computers and is able to download information into a pen drive or a CD. Some of the standard practices which many companies implement include disabling USB ports or disk drives. Also, restrictions on data transfer can be set in place, such as the requirement of administrator passwords for file copying and accessing shared folders.

For the average user, adding password protection to a computer is often enough to keep snoops out. Also, logging out of a session on a shared computer is a great way to avoid unwanted access to file folders. One common mistake is allowing a web browser to save the password to your accounts on a shared computer. If someone figures out your username, all they need to do is enter it, and the browser takes care of the rest.

Understanding access to data

One common practice is to assign levels of access to data. This means that certain data sets may have "open data," meaning that anyone within the organization, or with network access, may be able to see it. In other cases, the definition of open access may refer to certain information being of the public domain. This kind of information can be downloaded from a website or accessed by request. This kind of information may lack encryption in order to facilitate access.

"Restricted data" refers to data that is not freely available to all users. Now, the definition of "restricted" is rather broad in the sense that it may only apply to users with network access, or it might be restricted to users with password access. This is commonly found in shared folders and cloud-based storage applications. These data sets may also have some kind of encryption attached to it, thus limiting the abilities of unwanted users to read the information.

Lastly, "confidential data" is the type that contains sensitive information of an organization. In this type of data, there are extreme security measures attached to it, including high-level encryption and password access. This type of data may also be stored in "secret" drives and folders, which only a limited number of users have access to.

By understanding the tiers of sensitivity attached to data, you can take the appropriate measures that you need in order to protect your files and sensitive information. One such example, "confidential data" could personal information belonging to customers while "open data" may be information about the products and services that a company offers to its customers.

Network security best practices

Here are the best practices which you can put into practice when looking to protect your data.

- Take control of physical access points such as USB and disk drives.
- Don't neglect password restrictions to any sensitive information, folders, and drives.
- Ensure that access to wireless networks is protected by password access while wired connections are accessible to only those users who have permission to use them.
- Avoid the use of external pen drives, disks, and any other media which has not been previously scanned or cleared.
- The usage of high-level encryption will ensure that your data is bulletproof.
- Avoid the exchange of information over open networks or hotspots; these could be prone to packet sniffing.
- Shut down network access if there is a suspected network breach.
- Update passwords regularly (once a month is a good rule of thumb).

- Discourage password sharing among co-workers.
- It is better to spring a little extra for top-level encryption in order to ensure that confidential data is safe even if intercepted.

On the whole, network security is a matter of ensuring that you have the proper procedures in place. Also, it is important to have a clear idea of what to do in case of a data or security breach. Most firewalls and antivirus programs will offer functionalities that will alert you of coming from an unknown source. In general terms, these alerts happen in real-time. Consequently, you will have the opportunity to promptly shut down any potential attacks on your network.

Chapter 9: Wireless Technology and Security

Fully functional wireless networks and devices seemed like a dream a decade ago. In fact, many experts in the field did not believe that that entire computer networks could be run on wireless connections. Yet, the dependence on wired connections has been drastically reduced over the last few years. Nowadays, great deals of networks are run on wireless connections. For instance, cellphone communications are run entirely on wireless communications. Everything from calls to internet access; there is no need for any wired connections.

In a nutshell, a wireless network is a connection among devices that does not require the use of cables to connect the devices, either to the network or amongst themselves. In that sense, wireless networks offer a high degree of flexibility and simplicity as the physical limitations of having to install large amounts of wires, and cabling is not needed. In addition, the network can span over longer distances and does not demand that users be physically present in a given location in order to gain access to the network.

At present, wireless networks have simplified both access and mobility. Users can be on the move constantly and not miss a beat. This has enabled a multitude of users to experience new ways of communicating, especially when moving away for long distances. Indeed, wireless technology has revolutionized the way we interact with the world around us.

However, the use of wireless connections has also opened up a new set of threats and considerations which need to be taken into account. In general, wireless access requires both providers and users to exercise increased security practices. This is a stark contrast to a traditional wired connection.

With wired connections, unauthorized users needed to have access to both a physical terminal and a port to connect to. This means that breaking into the network itself was a rather complex task. Of course, an authorized user could perform a remote hack by gaining access through the use of a username and password. But most times, there had to be someone physically present in order to gain access to the network itself.

This aspect of wired networks is lost in wireless communications. Anyone within range of the Wi-Fi signal can potentially gain access to the network. This is why free Wi-Fi hotspots can become so unsafe for the average user. The fact of the matter is that anyone can gain access to the network, especially if it lacks encryption or the use of authentication.

As a result, security experts advocate the use of authentication either by means of a username and password, or a captive portal in the case of hotspots. Furthermore, encryption is highly recommended in order to avoid potential loss of information due to a package interception. With that in mind, most home networks are rather safe; that is, a typical residential network that provides wireless internet access to a group of devices is rather safe from unwanted users. Yet, there is always the risk of someone being on the prowl looking to find a vulnerable network.

In the case of business networks, wireless access needs to offer a greater degree of security. In many cases, enterprises deal with sensitive and confidential information. What this means is that network administrators need to ensure that unwanted users stay as far away as possible. Still, employees need to gain access to the network so that they can perform their day to day functions. With this in mind, awareness of the need to protect access to such connections truly becomes of the utmost importance.

What to Consider When Setting up a Wireless Connection

First and foremost, security is the biggest concern for wireless networks. In a world in which information is power, having access to information is a valuable commodity. As such, the question of security boils down to access to information and not access to the network itself. This means that the biggest concern in the mind of network administrators is not that unwanted users log on to the network; their biggest concern is that by logging on to the network, unwanted users will be privy to potentially sensitive information.

In that regard, restricting access to unwanted users in the number one priority for network administrators. Simple measures such as making sure that all users have an username and password are often enough to stifle the average hacker.

The next item that network administrators look to when setting up their wireless networks is simplicity. Simplicity implies the ease with which users can log on to the network and then use it to complete their objectives. With that in mind, administrators need to consider the bandwidth that will be required in order to accommodate the number of users on that particular network.

Often, it is easy to underestimate the requisite bandwidth. In fact, it is quite common for an administrator to estimate a given bandwidth and then realize that it is not enough to handle a full load. Other times, an administrator might make an appropriate assessment of the bandwidth that is required for the current load of users but does not take into account future users. Therefore, it is essential that an administrator consider both present and future bandwidth requirements.

Another important aspect to consider is the actual, physical infrastructure that is needed to produce the wireless network or provide Wi-Fi access to users. This physical infrastructure comes in the way of routers and signal extenders. The most challenging part of the physical infrastructure is directing the signal to where users will be. This can be a potential headache when homes and buildings are designed in a free-flowing style. Wi-Fi signals can often get stuck going around corners or up and downstairs. Even concrete buildings can absorb the signal rather than reflect to the devices that will connect.

One other key consideration when setting up a wireless network understands the devices that will connect to it. For example, if the network will mainly consist of smartphones and tablets, then a larger number of devices can be accommodated on to the network. In contrast, if a large number of PCs (which tend to be hungrier for bandwidth) connect to the network, then arrangements need to be made in order to accommodate the larger number of devices.

On the whole, setting up a wireless network is far easier than a standard wired connection. The configuration of software is less complex while there is a definite saving in terms of money; there are far fewer components to purchase and cabling that needs to be installed.

So, if you are looking to set up a network that won't break the bank and will allow multiple users to long on easily, then a wireless network can certainly fulfill those needs.

Drawbacks of a wireless network

For all its merits, a wireless network also poses a series of drawbacks that need to be taken into account. For starters, Wi-Fi access is far less reliable than wired access. The main reason for this is that signal strength on wireless networks fluctuates a lot more on wireless connections than it does on wired connections. In fact, there are many factors that can influence the quality of a wireless connection's signal strength. Factors such as the weather or interference from other devices (phones, TVs, and radios) may play into reducing the quality of a wireless signal. As a result, close monitoring of signal quality is essential in order to ensure the proper functioning of the network.

Another drawback is the connection's speed. Generally speaking, a wired connection will always run a lot faster than a wireless one. The reason for this is that a Wi-Fi signal can disperse throughout the environment where it is located. In the case of a wired connection, it has nowhere else to go, but the cable where it is being transmitted. This is what makes wired connections a lot more reliable and faster than wireless ones.

Also, wireless connections are dependent on the wireless adapter used by the devices that are connecting to the network. So, even if the network is reliable and free from obstructions, devices that do not have a solid and functional wireless adapter may actually experience decreased performance. Therefore, it is important to ensure that the devices connecting to the network have the best available wireless hardware.

As you can see, wireless networks, even with their drawbacks, offer a serviceable solution to virtually all residential users and most enterprises. Ultimately, the network administrator, or home user, needs to determine if the characteristics of a wireless network meet their needs, or if a wired network might be more suitable. Yet, wireless networks offer a good solution across the board.

Types of wireless networks and connections

Thus far, we have focused on wireless networks under the assumption that the network is designed to connect to the internet. This assumption is valid since the vast majority of networks will require some kind of internet access at some point. Most of the time, the reason for the network is so that it can connect to the internet.

Yet, there are other types of wireless connections that devices can use to communicate with each other.

To start off, Bluetooth is a common tool used to connect a small number of devices together. Usually, it consists of two devices that are paired with each other—a common example of this wireless headphone connected to a smartphone. Also, a printer can connect to a computer, or the phone may synch with a computer and so on.

Bluetooth is far slower than other types of wireless communication. Yet, it is useful for linking devices that aren't too far apart. Perhaps the biggest drawback is security as Bluetooth connections don't have much in the way of encryption to speak of. So, a skilled hacker may be able to connect to a device which happens to have Bluetooth enabled.

Beyond a run-of-the-mill Bluetooth connection, wireless networks can be rather simple and straightforward, or they can get rather complex.

A Wireless Local Area Network (WLAN) can be set up to enable communication among a small number of computers with or without access to the internet. In most cases, WLANs will have some form of access to the internet. Although, very confidential connections may be confined to a small workgroup using a WLAN without necessarily having access to the internet. In fact, there may be a separate WLAN that does have internet access. That way, the risk of a security breach can be limited. This type of connection can be limited to a home, individual office, or perhaps an entire building.

The next level is a Wireless Wide Area Network (WWAN). In this type of network, there is a much larger area to be covered. If the physical area exceeds the usual range of a wireless network, internet access may be required in order to join multiple connections. This type of connection can be used to link larger geographical areas, such as several city blocks.

A larger type of network is known as a Wireless Metropolitan Area Network (WMAN). This is the kind of network that can be used to link an entire city. Unless there are several repeater points that can distribute the signal over large physical areas, the most effective way to connect devices over a large area is to link them over the internet. In that case, any number of users can log on to the network as the need may be.

WMANs are used to connect entire cities. These are the types of networks that are used by large organizations. For instance, companies with several locations spread out over a city may rely on this type of configuration to help them manage communication among all of their users. These networks are also commonly used for commercial purposes such as advertising and broadcasting information.

One important factor that all of these connections have in common is that there is a central hub from which the signal is generated. This hub then sends out the signal to the various devices that will connect to it. Also, repeaters and signal extenders may be used in order to ensure that the signal covers the entire physical space that the administrator is looking to grant access.

Based on this logic, an ad-hoc connection is one that is set up without any kind of planning. For example, a laptop computer uses Bluetooth to connect a wireless printer and a smartphone. Then, the network will be disbanded once the tasks are complete. Another good example is when a smartphone is used as a wireless hotspot. In this case, the phone enables various devices to connect to it and thereby access the internet. Once the need for internet access is gone, then the network is disbanded.

As you can see, an ad-hoc network serves a very specific purpose, and then when it is no longer required, it disappears. Experienced users are good at building ad-hoc networks from scratch, either to help them when they are in a tough spot, or as a means of streamlining work.

Lastly, a hybrid connection is a kind that combines both wired and wireless access. This kind of network is commonly seen in enterprise settings. This type of network addresses all of the needs of a company in that wired connections are generally used for desktop PCs, while wireless connections are used for laptops and mobile devices.

Furthermore, a hybrid network offers a combination of mobility and security. Secure connections can be achieved on the wired connection while the wireless network can provide mobility to users. Since wireless connections tend to be less reliable than wired ones, the most sensitive tasks and information is carried out over the wired connection leaving less complex and sensitive tasks to the wireless network.

Other Uses of Wireless Technology

In the past, more rudimentary wireless technology such as shortwave radios provided the opportunity to connect over certain distances, especially when traditional broadcasting was unavailable. To this day, shortwave radios are essentially used by emergency broadcast systems and aficionados. However, this type of technology is still seen in law enforcement and emergency crews. While shortwave technology does not have a great deal of range, it is often enough to cover larger areas such as a medium-sized city.

Also, traditional radio communications are a great alternative since they provide users with the ability to connect without having the need for an expensive setup. With that in mind, users don't have to rely on the internet or even electrical energy to communicate.

As a matter of fact, military-grade radios use solar-powered cells to recharge batteries. This enables military units to remain operational for extended periods of time, especially when deployed in battle. These types of radios are also used in marine communications as well as airborne surveillance.

In addition, companies that have many of moving parts use radios to communicate among its various parts. Trucking companies, factories, and warehouses all use some type of radio communication to stay in the loop. Hospitals and emergency services utilize radio communications as a means of ensuring capabilities.

Radio technology has also been applied to what is now known as Radio Frequency Identification (RFID). This type of technology is used as a wireless network mainly deployed to identify and track units such as people, animals and vehicles. It is commonly used by trucking and cab companies to keep tabs on their vehicles.

Additionally, researchers use RFID to track animals in the wild.

There are two parts to an RFID system, an emitter and a receiver. The emitter, or transmitter, sends out a radio frequency that is picked up by the receiver. The receiver can then translate that signal into a digital signal which can be utilized to track movements on a map or pinpoint the location of a unit. This system has been deployed in search and rescue operations as well as scientific research.

Some critics of RFID claim that it is used to surveil individuals illegally. However, there is no conclusive evidence of its use outside of tracking people and objects for legitimate purposes. For example, people who are under house arrest that must wear an ankle bracelet have an RFID system attached to them. This allows law enforcement to determine their position in case they choose to flee.

One other interesting application of wireless technology can be seen in satellite communications. Traditional cellular telephony makes use of the Global System for Mobile (GSM) network. This network uses a SIM card with a unique ID on it to identify a mobile phone number. This enables the mobile phone to place calls and have access to the internet.

However, in the case of satellite communication, mobile receivers and transmitters don't necessarily use the traditional GSM network. In fact, they may bypass this system altogether and connect to any of the other communications satellites in the Earth's orbit. These so-called satellite phones have coverage in virtually all corners of the Earth.

One great example of this kind of communication is military Satcom. Harris radios, for instance, use UHF and VHF frequencies to communicate among aircraft and seaborne vessels. Ultra-high frequency (UHF) and Very High Frequency (VHF), can be used to triangulate communication between an airborne vessel and a ground crew. Given the advancements in this type of technology, aircrews can send live video in HD to ground crews who can then assess a situation as seen from the aircraft.

This type of technology has been widely employed for aerial reconnaissance, for example, in border protection, as well as, search and rescue and disaster relief. There is also a weather application for the use of the technology through the use of Unmanned Aerial Vehicles (UAV). These types of vehicles can track weather patterns to a point where a manned crew would never be able to reach. All of the communications are relayed from the aircraft up to the satellite and then broadcast back down to the ground crew. Likewise, the ground crew can then communicate with the aircraft in mid-flight.

These examples all show how wireless communications have a plethora of applications. There ensure that communication does not breakdown and can be maintained over vast areas of physical space. While the more robust capabilities of such wireless communication is reserved for the domain of military and law enforcement, civilian applications have led to the mapping of remote areas of the planet and the discovery of previously unknown features of the Earth.

One of the most common issues that arise when discussing UHF and VHF communications is encryption. It should be noted that these types of networks use military-grade encryption, meaning that it uses the most robust algorithms known to date. These algorithms are essentially impossible to crack since they would require a vast amount of computing power that the average hacker would never be able to procure.

If you are keen on using these types of communication networks, there are civilian versions of satellite phones which can be purchased freely. They come with a subscription that grants access to the network of satellites that orbit the Earth. They are essentially the same satellites that the military uses. However, you would not have access to the same channels and frequencies that the military does.

The Global Positioning System

The Global Positioning System (GPS) is essentially a wireless network that is used as a navigation aid. It is used in all types of transportation. In fact, it is so common nowadays that most smartphones come equipped with a GPS application that enables users to pinpoint any location on the planet.

One great example of such application is Google Maps. This application can help drivers navigate practically any city in the world with frightening accuracy. Technically, this application does not need internet access since it uses its satellite link and not its internet signal. Yet, the application does not function appropriately since it uses an internet connection to download maps for its current location. What this means is that your phone determines your location by using the GPS network, but needs internet access to download the map for that location.

Google Street View is an example of how accurate satellite mapping can be. The satellite orbiting the Earth can literally take pictures of an average street while it is hundreds of miles above. This is certainly an incredible and very useful feature.

The GPS system uses the same system as Satcom or GSM technology. It essentially works in a triangulation system, that is, the satellite, the receiver, and the tower. This triangulation is what enables the pinpointing of precise locations.

In the case of marine applications in which there are no towers in the middle of the ocean, GPS can maintain triangulation by using other satellites in orbit. This is why military applications of the GPS system enable units to navigate any corner of the world. For the average user though, GPS is a lifesaver when driving in a new city or through an unknown path.

Bringing it all together

Wireless networks are here to stay. They make linking devices, and by extension users, a lot easier than through traditional wired connections. For all of the ease of use and mobility, questions about the overall reliability of wireless networks still abound. The fact of the matter is that this is technology which is yet to be perfected. What this means is that there are bugs still to be worked out.

As far as the average user is concerned, wireless has come a long way. Most cell carriers have a decent record of reliability. So, unless there is a natural disaster that disrupts coverage, wireless networks are usually reliable.

The other aspect of wireless networks is security. High-level encryption has increased information security tremendously over the last few years. In fact, standard encryption, as offered by free web-based e-mail servers, is good enough to keep the average intruder away from your information. There are more robust subscription services out there that offer closet to military-grade encryption. These services are commonly used by companies and individuals who handle a great deal of sensitive information.

On the whole, wireless technology is easy to use and very flexible. It will certainly meet the needs of the average user while enabling more advanced users to get their job done. By following the security guidelines which we have outlined earlier in this book, you can rest assured that your information will be safe from the attacks of unscrupulous folks. After all, hackers love to feed off low hanging fruit. They generally run away from a serious challenge. Thus, you can make it hard for them by beefing up your security measures.

Chapter 10: Introduction to Machine Learning: A Computer Networking Perspective

What is Machine Learning?

The above analogy is merely intended to draw our attention to the primary topic issue that concerns this study session: machine learning.

Can computers really learn? Better still, can they learn from their experiences with the different tasks that they handle on a day-to-day basis? Machine learning is a discipline that can sufficiently provide answers to the above questions.

In a layman's language, machine learning can be described as a process of acquiring skills that have been accumulated over time through observation. We can deduct from this simple description that machine learning starts by observation. The observation goes for a certain period.

In the process of observing, skills are acquired while others are sharpened, even further-learning from experience. This is one example of a normal human's learning throughout their time here on planet earth.

A more concrete definition of a machine does exist. Let's say that machine is a process that involves the acquisition of specialized skill(s) computed/accumulated from data over a period of time. Still, this sounds like we're talking about humans.

But we need to talk about machine learning in terms of machine 'behavior', and more specifically, as regards computers.

In Computing Terms

Machine learning is classified as a subset of Artificial Intelligence. As a subset of Artificial Intelligence, machine learning entails the development of algorithms that enable computers to learn from accumulated data and functions performed in the past. This concept was conceived in 1959 by Arthur Samuel.

Sample historical data (training data) offer a basis for machine learning algorithms to deliver models that aid in decision-making as well as predictions. This is done without any explicit programming.

Creative predictive models are products of the union between statistics and computer science.

How Machine Learning Works

Machine learning system achieves its mandate by following the following steps:

- A thorough examination of (or learning from) historical data that has accumulated over a given period.
- The building of prediction models.
- Prediction of output (on reception of new data).

The amount of data largely determines how accurate the predicted output turns out to be. A huge sample of historical is necessary for creating better prediction models that guarantee the high accuracy of predicted output.

Features of Machine Learning

The following are the main characteristics of Machine Learning:

- The use of data for pattern detection in datasets.
- Automatic improvement after learning from historical data.
- Machine learning is technologically data-driven.
- It has appreciable similarities with data mining-dealing with huge data amounts.

Why Machine Learning?

There is a day-by-day increase in the need for machine learning. One key factor for embracing machine learning with unimaginable seriousness as it is now, obviously, is the ability of machines to handle tasks that are highly sophisticated, better than humans. We can read, understand, and interpret data, but we are only limited to a few megabytes of data. Machines can handle terabytes of data, or even more, with a lot of accuracy.

With machine learning, the world can now boast of self-driven cars. Friend suggestion on social media platforms is also real, thanks to machine learning. Furthermore, face recognition, among other big advancements, are outcomes after big strides in machine learning.

In summary, the need for machine learning is anchored on the following key observations:

- Increment and rapid production of data, in respect of the widespread adoption of information systems.
- Handling highly sophisticated tasks that are practically impossible to a human being.
- Critical decision-making needs with regards to large and complex data or information. For instance, in finance and economics projections for individual businesses, companies, the machine is trained on pattern prediction therefrom and eventually gives a prediction on that basis. And even governments.

- Extracting patterns and information that are not easily visible to the human eye.

Classification of machine learning

Machine learning is classified as follows:

Reinforcement learning: this is a feedback-based mode of learning. A learning agent (machine) is penalized for every wrong pattern prediction and undesirable outcome. On the other hand, the same learning agent (machine) is rewarded for a job well done.

Unsupervised learning: a machine trains on outcome prediction without any supervision. Given data sets are not labeled, but the machine has to learn and eventually predict an outcome. Unsupervised machine learning is categorized into clustering and association.

Supervised learning: labeled data is provided to a machine. The machine is trains on pattern prediction therefrom and eventually gives a prediction on that basis.

There are two categories of supervised learning: classification and regression.

Machine Learning Applications

Machine learning is a crucial to each, and every sector being it economic, social, or administrative sector. Thus, the application of machine learning can be summarized under the following three key areas:

Machine Learning in Analytics

Statistics is every aspect of life. Sometimes we use it without knowing that we're actually using it. For instance, a person who wonders about a terrible experience would expectedly learn from it and take a totally different course of action given similar circumstances. Knowingly or otherwise, the person assesses the different events leading to a particularly horrible incident against what would have led to a different turn of events. The process may seem straightforward, but the truth is there is a lot of analytical work happening in the busy mind of the victim.

In normal life, politics invest so much in statistics to gauge the popularity of political candidates and help in making crucial political decisions. Similarly, all sectors use statistical results based on historical data to predict various events in the future.

Machine learning takes up this whole business to a whole new level by eliminating so much of human effort by merely allowing algorithms to analyze data and offer a prediction of patterns and likely outcome based on accumulated data.

Machine Learning in Management

Management rely heavily on statistical data in decision-making. In business, the management is charged with the responsibility of making decisions regarding employ recruitment and laying off; employ remunerations; budgetary projections; and the structure of leadership within a given organization or institution. In formal settings, such decisions are not arrived at hastily or without thought. In most cases, it takes months or even years to analyze relevant masses of data before deciding what is good for the organization or institution. With machine learning, the analysis of such data is more efficient since machines have the ability to handle huge data amounts that would otherwise take years to be done by a human. In fact, some analytical work is way beyond the ability of the smartest man on earth.

Machine Learning in Security

Security has been enhanced greatly with the adoption of machine learning systems. CCTV cameras, metal detectors, security alarms, and other security devices are perfect examples of machine learning in use. For instance, face recognition services are particularly important in ATM machines since they massively add to the security of ATM centers.

In summary, machine learning is an important subset of artificial intelligence, especially during the present times when we have to deal with a lot of data and information as a result of the information systems euphoria. Healthcare, financial sector, education sector and and governments need statistical data to make crucial decisions for sustainable operations. With machine learning, such needs can be met more efficiently.

Conclusion

A computer network can comprise of two computers. As long as the computers are connected, can communicate and share resources, the network is complete. However, there is no limit as far as the number of networked computers. The internet is a perfect example of how big a network can be.

Resource sharing and communication are the two biggest functions of a network. But that does not mean there is not much beyond communication and sharing of resources on the computer. In fact, many people make connections to the internet merely for entertainment. Others get linked to networks for collaborative work, research, and many other tasks.

Networks, notably, do not comprise of computers alone. There are a lot of other network components that make computers much more interesting. Printers, cables, routers, and many other hardware devices add to computer networks' collection of important hardware requirements. Besides, software applications and network protocols all gang up to make computer networks what they really are.

As important as computer networks are, running and managing them is never a walk in the park. Network security is one concern that gives concerned network users and administrators sleepless nights. Networks attacks are real, and they pose serious threats to the security and safety of user information as well as network resources. Being in the position to deal with network threats effectively is key to maintaining the integrity of the network.

In summary, computer networks are invaluable assets that must be guarded keenly. They make communication more effective besides offering a platform for many other important functions. In this IT-oriented era, computer networking is the key to effective communication, research, and collaboration.

Made in the USA
Las Vegas, NV
14 January 2021